China as a Model of Development

CHINA
AS A MODEL OF
DEVELOPMENT

AL IMFELD

Translated by Matthew J. O'Connell

Library of Congress Cataloging in Publication Data

Imfeld, Al, 1935-
    China as a model of development.

    Translation of China als Entwicklungsmodell.
    Bibliography: p.
    1. China—Politics and government—1949-
2. China—Economic conditions—1949-
3. China—Social conditions. I. Title.
JQ1508.I4413   309.1'51'05   76-4827
ISBN 0-88344-053-9   (cloth)

Paperbound Edition, 1977
Paperbound ISBN 0-88344-051-2

Originally published as *China als Entwicklungsmodell* by Imba
Verlag, Avenue de Beauregard 4, CH-1701 Freiburg, Switzer-
land

This translation copyright © 1976 Orbis Books, Maryknoll,
New York 10545

Manufactured in the United States of America

CONTENTS

3.96-orbis

Introduction

CHINA AS A MODEL

The China of Mao Tse-tung was cut off from the rest of the world for over two decades. During that period it was not solely the fault of the Chinese that the average Westerner knew nothing of China or knew only its cruel and negative side. Even for the United Nations "China" meant only the small island of Taiwan. Officially, the world had no knowledge of the vast continental China with its more than six million square miles of territory and seven hundred million inhabitants.

Now China has re-opened its doors to the rest of the world. The change has come at a time when both the East and West are in ferment and approaching a crisis, and when the Third World countries, after initial great enthusiasm, are becoming increasingly disenchanted with the development process as it presently exists. Eastern, Western, and non-aligned blocs—industrialized and underdeveloped countries alike—are ready for a reflective pause in the wild race for economic growth and constant technological gains.

The timing is fortuitous because China, as the rest of the world is discovering, has taken a different path toward development. China has turned inward, deliberately concentrated on agriculture, and taken only careful steps toward industrialization. And almost uniquely China began with the spiritual root of things: It first won the masses and then, with their new spirit and outlook, undertook the process of development cooperatively. And having worked together, with the courage to limit their own desires, the Chinese people have now reached the point where they can point to vast accomplishments.

In 1949 hunger was still a constant threat to the vast majority of the Chinese people. Since then the Chinese have channeled rivers and streams, drained swamps, terraced the land and cultivated it, and laid down irrigation systems. In the process, millions of square meters of new land have been acquired. Today every Chinese can have enough to eat at any time. This fact alone represents a great gain for China, particularly in comparison with most of the other developing countries.

In 1949, about 70 percent of the rural population possessed no land of their own. Now these people are all grouped in communes, sharing ownership and taking part in the planning of their own future.

In 1949, the majority of peasants and workers were uninformed, uneducated, and illiterate. Now they are involved in an ongoing process of consciousness-raising, have been "politicized," and have, through projects geared to the masses, become literate enough for their needs.

In short: China is still poor, still a developing nation, but its poverty is mitigated, shared by all, and filled with the hope that the continuing revolution will conquer the irrationality of nature and the innate reluctance of society to change.

They are only initial successes, yet the accomplishments are all the more overwhelming when one remembers that almost all the one hundred other developing nations, despite massive help from West and East, are still far from having achieved any of them.

The Chinese readily admit that they are far from having reached their own goal, and that there have often been—and still are—moments when the whole structure threatened to collapse and the wheels seemed to have stopped. Still and all, as John Kenneth Galbraith writes: "It is the Chinese future. And let there be no doubt: for the Chinese it works" (*Observer* [London], July 1, 1973).

In the eyes of both the Chinese themselves and Western visitors, their experiment is still a model, a plan, a point of reference not always a reality. Much in it belongs to the realm of ideas, of the future, of hope and vision.

But for the rest of the world this Chinese model should be a stimulus to an examination of conscience. Its example and the contrast with other developing countries enable us to see other possibilities and paths to follow. Neville Maxwell, a well-known journalist and expert on China, expresses this idea of model by saying: "China is more important to the world as an idea than as a place" (*Sunday Times* [London], February 13, 1972).

From the viewpoint of the politics of development the Chinese way is a real challenge. Given today's disenchantment in both the industrialized and the developing countries, we must ask whether the Chinese have not found a better way to get at the roots of underdevelopment.

In the eyes of Mao and those who think as he does, the vast majority of the peoples of Asia, Africa, and Latin America face the same problem the Chinese Communist Party faced during its original twenty-two year struggle (1927–1949). China, therefore, is a model or path which these other peoples should carefully study. However, the Chinese insist that their way cannot be taken over without modification; Mao himself has warned other countries on this point. The Chinese model cannot simply be copied, any more than the Western model can simply be transplanted to the developing countries. The Chinese are well aware of this. They think of themselves, therefore, as simply an idea or model for the Third World to profit by.

The aim of the following chapters is not to glorify China. My only concern is to isolate certain important factors which have made it possible for China to rouse an exhausted people and weld them into a

4

truly developing nation in a little over two decades. I aim to show what China's starting point was, what it stressed, and how it set about the process of development.

The really interesting thing about China for the rest of us is how it has attempted to solve the immense problems blocking its development. China has engaged in a series of solutions, but what it accomplished is not, in itself, the most important thing for outsiders. My concern is to take its successes and to use them in formulating a new theory of development. The value of the Chinese model is to show what development can be and how it can take place.

I am very much aware of the subjective element in my judgment. Each of us sees China differently; the spectrum of reactions ranges all the way from horror to hope. One person sees the China he dreams of, another the China he fears. But this very range of reactions indicates to me that we cannot ignore China and that it has some value as a model for everyone. China today is less a brute fact than a symbol. China's spark, to use Mao's words, "can start a prairie fire."

1

A FAITH THAT MOVES MOUNTAINS

The Chinese revolution, like every other, sprang from a new faith and a powerful hope. No one takes the burdensome and often terrible road of revolution simply in order to end up with the old hierarchies, repressions, and exploitations in a new dress.

The real incitement to revolution in China was the hope of equality and brotherhood. For many of us in the West these words have degenerated into slogans, and we react to them with skepticism. A visitor to today's China, however, soon realizes that there the promise of these words has given rise to an authentic popular movement. The hope of equality has become an explosive force for social revolution.

Western visitors to present-day China are always surprised to meet happy, satisfied Chinese, people

7

who have a certain radiance about them. Such an attitude can only be rooted in the realization that life, work, even poverty and self-denial, have a meaning.

The United States Secretary of State, Henry Kissinger, was once asked why the Chinese impressed him so deeply. His answer: "Because they have a *Weltanschauung*. The rest of us have lost our way . . . (our) vision" (*Newsweek*, March 26, 1973).

The true spirit of the Chinese social revolution is best expressed as the near-universal will to serve the people. The revolution has really brought into existence a new spirit—almost a new spirituality; Mao Tse-tung has succeeded in imbuing every Chinese with the meaning and importance of service so that today every Chinese, whether he be a civil servant or a factory worker, is proud of the work he does.

In developing this spirit, Mao was able to use tradition for his starting point. As John K. Fairbank, Sinologist at Harvard University, points out, the Chinese are the "most socially minded human beings among the peoples of the world. . . " (*Newsweek*, February 21, 1972). Confucianism and Taoism had taught the Chinese to see themselves always as part of a whole, a people or a state. The simple peasant, therefore, knows that he is promoting his own good when he serves the people; he realizes that if the whole possesses coherence and harmony, then he himself will have order, peace, and happiness.

8

But Mao introduced one important change. He linked the idea of equality to that of service, thus removing service from its old vertical or hierarchical context and situating it on a horizontal or egalitarian level. In China today, to serve the people means to regard all as equal, to be at the disposal of one another.

The Chinese have taken every means possible to keep this new spirit of service and equality intensely alive and to revitalize it from time to time. In similar fashion we Westerners continually create an atmosphere that will promote production and consumption. Anyone traveling from Hong Kong to Canton becomes very much aware of the similarities and contrasts between China and the Westernized world. In Hong Kong, loudspeakers, neon lights, and newspaper ads urge the citizenry to buy Coca-Cola, Sony radios, Mercedes-Benz automobiles, or flights on TWA and invite the passerby into hotels, bars, movie houses, and dance halls. In Canton, too, one hears and sees slogans, advertisements, and wall newspapers, but here they are given over to moral imperatives affecting the life and activity of the populace: "Serve the people!" "Have the courage to think and act!" "Politics first!" "Away with the bourgeois mentality; make the proletarian ideology your own."

The Chinese do not, however, simply have a lot of slogans; they also have an enthusiasm that puts those slogans into practice. Mao's wish has been fulfilled: "What we need is an attitude of prudent

9

enthusiasm, and action that is intensive but orderly." Over and over, one hears "Fight against individualism and self-interest!" Every visitor is amazed at the zeal with which the Chinese work for the common good. "Forget yourself and think of others" truly runs like a refrain through all aspects of life. In other words, what seem to be mere slogans are more than that: They are a profession of faith and a force that can "move mountains."

The revolution has not simply destroyed an ancient social system. It has also changed the consciousness of an entire people. To the Westerner exhortations to "serve the people" or "put politics first" may seem shopworn, but to the individual Chinese they give the sense that he is taking part in a vast constructive program. According to the Maoist faith, a transformation of thinking also expands a person's possibilities and capacity for work, his creative power and inventiveness. Thus an inner change in society is even able to effect a transformation in nature itself. It was the "red revolution" that made the "green revolution" possible.

Two examples serve to show how this new faith of the Chinese can "move mountains" and "work miracles," just as the Christian and Moslem faiths once did. (The two expressions are constantly used in the official weekly, the *Peking Review*.)

In the village of Tachai (which, as the report notes, is often used as a model in the new China):

Civil servants of long experience must attend special "May Seventh Cadres' Schools" in order to get rid of their "official manner"; intellectuals with highly specialized training must learn from the peasants how to till the soil. The purpose of these various campaigns is to produce a Communist "all-around person" who is as familiar with spade and dung-fork as with computer or surgical instruments. At the same time, the effort is made to root out egoism and concern with a personal career. "Hard work" for the revolutionary cause— without regard to whether or not the work one does is pleasant—is the main concern in all activity. The village of Tachai is a model of what can be achieved in this way. Here a commune was able, by its own resources and without any outside assistance, to build terraces and fields on steep, uncultivated slopes; the yield of these fields increases each year. The building of electrically powered funicular railways, tractors, electric mills, etc., all with local resources and under local supervision is impressive evidence of the power of the commune. Tachai is a model for all of China [*Orientierung*, February 15, 1972].

In the Lingsien District, Honan Province, Central China:

Residents. . . have completed an achievement unique in the history of the People's Republic.

In 10 years of work, communal farmers, labourers, and soldiers have transformed mountainous, unfertile scrubland into a model agricultural area supporting a population of 700,000.

Today a canal system spreads through the Taihang mountain chain, which at times reaches 5,200 ft. The Red Flag canal winds through 134 tunnels with a total length of 15 miles and, with the help of 150 aqueducts, connects with remote areas where a decade ago not a drop of water could be found. With all its branches, the canal is more than 950 miles long.

And to connect it with the nearest river—the Tschang-ho in Shansi Province—one reservoir and 15 bridges had to be cleared away, often under unspeakable hardship and difficulty. About 580 million cubic feet of rock and soil was removed.

Where formerly there was not food for a single mountain goat, farmers are today growing wheat, raising sheep, and attempting to produce rice. Terraced fields have been built, and in the valleys are fruit and walnut trees [*Guardian*, May 17, 1972].

Edgar Snow, who possessed an exceptional grasp of Mao's thinking, sums up the whole vision in his posthumously published *The Long Revolution*:

To speed up the erasure of differences between town and countryside; to move toward closer equalization of material and cultural standards and opportunities of the worker, the peasant, the soldier, the cadre, and the technician-expert; to integrate shop and classroom work in everyone's education and life-experience; to smash all bourgeois thought and especially its remnants among intellectuals and officials; to proletarianize higher learning by integrating students and workers and combining labor practice with classroom theory; to bring public health and medical services to the rural masses; to train everyone to bear arms and learn from the army; to create a one-class generation of many-sided, well-educated youths inspired by the ideals of service to the people, at home and abroad, contemptuous of personal wealth, and dedicated to a "world outlook" anticipating the final liberation of man from hunger, greed, ignorance, war, and capitalism [p. 21].

Application to Other Developing Countries

The Chinese are convinced that only such faith as theirs can lead to an authentic revolution and a corresponding spirituality. Indeed, the Chinese delegate to the United Nations Conference on Trade and Development at Santiago, Chile (UNCTAD III) said this is the only way by which the developing countries can make further progress. A new mentality, a new philosophy, a new faith, a new spirituality, or a new ideology is needed if a revolution is not to be simply a change in the tip of the iceberg. It is not enough merely to acquire the means and technology for development; the people must also acquire a new hope, and only faith can give that people the energy needed to bring that hope to fruition. Without faith, without vision there is only an artificial construct. It may be called "development," but that will be only a label; there will be no creative process.

2

BUILDING ON
THE PAST

For a long time Westerners simply misunderstood the Chinese Cultural Revolution. They
thought it was an effort to eradicate the past totally.
Harrowing descriptions in the Western press gave
the impression that everything which might recall
the old China was being destroyed, not only in the
museums but in the soul of the Chinese people. The
fear was abroad that the Chinese were being turned
into a people without a history, completely de-
prived of roots, hurled into anarchy and chaos, in
the hope that a new China would arise phoenix-like
out of the ashes.

It is undoubtedly true that during the Cultural
Revolution some masterpieces of art were destroyed. Most of these were pieces that had been
hoarded away by the nouveaux riches; they were

destroyed, amid deliberate publicity, as a warning not to let revolutionary energy flag. It is true, too, that at the very beginning of the Cultural Revolution the treasures of the past were locked up and had guards posted over them. And some works may have been deliberately sacrificed in order to make it clear that even the treasures of the past must be put at the service of the revolution.

However, the Chinese revolutionaries, Mao most of all, were well aware that when a people is so conscious of its history and has a proud tradition dating back thousands of years, no one can strip it, interiorly or exteriorly, of its heritage. Indeed, the history of the Chinese revolution makes it quite clear that its great power and success has come from deliberately bringing the dynamism characteristic of the past into creative tension with a vision of the future. Mao has known how to link the old with the new, how to renew the old by giving it the added dimension of the future and of the revolutionary impulse. He himself has always insisted both that "the old must be put to the service of the present" and that "the new must emerge from a critical acceptance of the old."

In his address on "Art and Literature" Mao says: "One of our tasks is to study our historical heritage and to understand it through the application of Marxist methods. Our national history covers several thousand years and has its own characteristics as well as countless treasures."

As a very young man Mao was gripped by enthusiasm for Westernization and fell under the influence of the father of the Chinese Revolution, Sun Yat-sen. But Mao was a peasant's son and soon found this solution of China's problem suspect. During his own protracted meditation on Marxism and Leninism and their significance for China, he also came under the influence of two other important thinkers, who challenged both the Western and the Russian forms of development. One was the librarian of Peking University, Li Ta-chao (born 1889), who hired the twenty-four-year-old Mao in 1918 as an assistant; the other was Kuo Mo-jo (born 1892), a Marxist-oriented scholar, who today is president of the Academy of Sciences at Peking and a personal friend of Mao.

Li Ta-chao added the element of populism to Russian Marxism. In an essay written in the winter of 1918/19, he stressed the moral superiority of the countryside over the city and assured his readers: "Our China is a rural nation, in which peasants form the majority of the working classes; as long as the peasants are not liberated, the nation as a whole will not be liberated!" This principle was to be the foundation on which Mao built his party and his revolution.

Kuo Mo-jo's thought is exemplified in his creation of an imaginary conversation between Confucius and Marx. It shows how the Chinese Marxists attempted to create a link with the past, and how the two worldviews, those of Confucius and Marx, are not contradictory. Simultaneously the writer says, in an ironic tone, neither Confucius nor Marx can provide a ready-made solution for the problems of modern China. Kuo Mo-jo's literary discussion is but one example of how the Chinese revolutionaries worked to transpose the past into the present in a critical way.

Maoism does indeed preserve a good deal more of the older thinking than has usually been realized. Theodor Leuenberger, historian at Sankt-Gallen, has pointed out the unity between the old and the new: "One thing is sure: The links between Chinese Communism and Chinese history are much closer than the outside may judge." And in a seven-hundred page book, Sinologist Wolfgang Bauer shows that the Chinese Revolution has brought to fulfillment the age-old Chinese "hope of happiness." Viewed thus, China's rich tradition becomes, as it were, its Old Testament.

Some scholars have even gone so far as to say that they see nothing new in Mao and his revolution. In fact, however, China's passage from the ancient tradition to the new has been as radical as was the passage from the Old Testament to the New. The old was brought to completion, and with the new a new era began. Writer Lin Yu-tang (born 1895) uses language clearly reminiscent of the Bible to show that Mao's teaching and deeds are bringing the ancient Chinese prophecies closer to fulfillment:

That time will come; the development has already begun; it is now permeating high and low alike, working as invisibly and yet irresistibly as the dawn breaking. A while yet disgust and torment will be masters, but then the stillness will come, and with it beauty and simplicity . . . and justice. And we today will seem only children of the dawn to the people that dwells in that land of justice.

Mao's historical revolutionary thinking has succeeded in renewing the ancient dynamism between Yang and Yin—the dynamic and the static, the masculine and the feminine. In the centuries preceding the revolution, one side of this tension, that represented by popular Confucianism, had become completely dominant, so that new ideas and energies based on Taoism and Buddhism had no chance of becoming effective. Confucianism was abused to become the mainstay of feudalism, of administrators, and of the ruling classes. In their view, everything new was a departure from the perfect order established by the past. In other words, Confucianism was used to justify the status quo and those who profited by it.

The theoreticians of China's new way went back to the traditions of Taoism and Buddhism. These traditions contain strong elements of the mystical and the magical, of charism and expectation of salvation, of folklore and egalitarianism. And precisely because this stream had so long been dammed up, once released it swept centuries of stagnation before it.

According to philologists, Taoist and Zen Buddhist symbols often appear in Mao's writing. His speech, too, is full of verbal symbols that have deep roots in the popular soul. Stuart R. Schram, an expert on Mao's writings, says that "he has created a synthesis between Marxism-Leninism and traditional China."

Yet another proof that new China does not regard tradition as antirevolutionary is its strong interest in archeology. Evidences of the past are carefully preserved and made accessible to the masses. Captions or oral commentaries explain how the people's work supplied the ancient rulers with valuable coffins, silk garments embroidered with beautiful motifs, and splendid porcelain. The point constantly emphasized is that these works of art owe their existence to the genius of the masses, and viewers are made indignantly aware that the feudal society of the past was able to possess such glorious masterpieces only through complete exploitation of the people.

One important reason why Mao's thinking has carried the day is that it has, by stimulating a carefully directed pride in the nation's past, strengthened a self-awareness that has revolutionary effects. Ancient treasures were found to contain a healing power, and they have helped the nation recover from the terrible scars of colonial and imperialist humiliation.

Application to Other Developing Countries

Many developing countries, especially those in Africa, are trying to create a development without historical foundations. In fact it is often the intention of developers to eradicate all memories of the past. The result is an attempt to build on nothing, with no contribution from the people and the stream of popular tradition; consequently, it has no coherence. In colonial times the history of the colonized nation was not taught, and students simply had the history of the colonists stuffed into them. Since that was the history of the oppressor, there was nothing in it to fire their pride.

But when development lacks continuity with the past—whether through ignorance of that past or through deliberate policy—it comes as something totally new and the masses can view it only with mistrust. China, on the contrary, has realized that even the study of history and the past can become a powerful force in shaping the future. Thus, one lesson to be drawn from the Chinese experience is that development and revolution must build on native tradition and history. As in the Christian religions the passage from the Old Testament to the New is the fulfillment of what had always been hoped for, so development must be the fulfillment of the past, not its destruction.

3

THE NEW NEED
NOT BE THE FOREIGN

After the Manchu dynasty had been overthrown in 1911, Sun Yat-sen, founder of the Kuomintang and first president of the Republic of China, believed that the modernization of China implied its Westernization. At the beginning of the century most Chinese intellectuals shared this view. They were convinced that China could survive as people, nation, and state only if it, like Japan, graduated from the school of Western civilization. The two chief spokesmen of this view were Hu Shih and Chen Tu-hsiu, who, in 1915, founded the magazine *New Youth*. In its first number Chen appealed to the young and insisted that China could stand fast against foreign aggressors only if it changed it social structure and thus made possible the kind of dynamic development seen in the West. A primary condition of this whole process was that personal initiative be given free rein. Chen was all for a radical Westernization of China; this meant democracy, science, personal initiative, unlimited competition, and the organization of the military and of civil life.

For Chen "the American and British spirit of enterprise, the German organizational genius, the scientific and revolutionary spirit of the French and Germans" were models which China must take to heart. So Chen and his fellow theoreticians promoted a cult of individuality and willpower.

Initially Mao was heavily influenced by this approach. Only gradually and after much bitter experience did he come to another view. Mao's predecessors equated the foreign with the new, but Mao finally took a different tack: He began to emphasize all that is natively Chinese and the continuity of his own and his country's history. By so doing he gained access to his own people.

Mao's initially vague ideas developed over time into a firm foundation of thought and action. China followed the Soviet model of development until 1956, despite numerous disillusionments. After splitting from Sun Yat-sen's school of thought, Mao first believed that China need reject only the capitalist West, but it became ever more clear to him that it could not follow the Soviet way either. As early as the 1930s he was hammering at the need for a "Chinese version of Marxism." In 1942, at the inauguration of the Central Party School at Yenan, he called for "the development of a theory that would apply to the real needs of China, a theory that would be our own and proper to us."

As a result of Mao's and his followers' reflections on these needs and through their determined efforts to come to grips with their own history, a new model of development has gradually been worked out. This model makes it no longer possible always to equate development with Westernization or following the example of the Soviet Union.

This non-Western model makes it very difficult for a Westerner to see present-day China as it really is or to pass any valid judgment on it. Only if we study the Chinese tradition and character can we come to understand Maoism. For what is new in the China of Mao Tse-tung does not come from the West and, therefore, cannot be evaluated according to Western standards. In other words, we must judge the Chinese according to their own norms, not ours.

The Chinese, for example, think in terms of "we," not of "I," and they act accordingly. For them individual freedom is not sacrosanct; their whole tradition leans much more than ours to thinking in terms of the community as a whole. Over and over in the course of China's history great masses of people have been summoned to forced labor. The building of the Great Wall, for example, required, according to tradition, the toil of 700,000 people, and we read of 100,000 laborers being ordered out for the laying of roads. Around the year 1375, the linking of the Yen River with the Great

Canal is supposed to have occupied 300,000 people for seven months. So, too, in recent years, mass labor and the principle of cooperation were called upon for the building of the dikes and irrigation systems needed for rice cultivation.

What is new in China has come into existence largely from the creative activity of the Chinese themselves. Precisely because China's development did not take the form of learning something foreign through practice, it could be placed at the service of the people and be brought about by their own efforts. The success of their efforts in turn fostered self-confidence and a legitimate pride. This kind of development has not led to feelings of inferiority and to dependence, but to self-sufficiency and freedom.

Application to Other Developing Countries

With a few exceptions, most other countries have seen development as modernization and Westernization. It has seldom been a process geared to the realities of the nation seeking it. There has been no tapping of the wisdom latent in the people, no drawing upon it for the work of development. All that has been done has been to copy and distort, to alienate and isolate. But China is proof that the new need not be the foreign.

4

THE NECESSARY
REVOLUTION

Despite its roots in history, the new China is by no means simply the result of a peaceful, smooth development. On the contrary, the achievement required a radical transformation, a genuine revolution. In a class society (such as the old China was) revolutions and revolutionary wars are inevitable. "Without them," Mao wrote in 1937, "it is impossible to make a leap forward in the development of society, to overturn the dominant reactionary classes, and to put the people into the position of power."

Indeed from the beginning of this century scarcely any Chinese intellectuals thought in terms of mere reform. All were convinced that an entirely new social structure was necessary. And all knew as well that such a transformation would not come easily. No one in power simply resigns; no class surrenders its privileges without a struggle. The huge masses of poor Chinese peasants (they constitute 70 percent of the population) were under the thumb of the feudal authorities. Winning rights and justice for these people was in itself a revolution, so that Mao could say, "Without the poor peasants there can be no revolution. To attack them is to attack the revolution."

Any regrouping of society on such a scale inevitably requires sacrifice—suffering, even death. Here, as elsewhere, Mao was a realist. In his "Report of an Investigation into the Peasant Movement in Hunan," he writes:

A revolution is not the same as inviting people to dinner, or writing an essay, or painting a picture, or doing fancy needlework; it cannot be anything so refined, so calm and gentle, or so mild, kind, courteous, restrained and magnanimous. A revolution is an uprising, an act of violence whereby one class overthrows another. A rural revolution is a revolution by which the peasantry overthrows the authority of the feudal landlord class. If the peasants do not use the maximum of their strength, they can never overthrow the authority of the landlords which has been deeply rooted for thousands of years. In the rural areas, there must be a great, fervent revolutionary upsurge, which alone can arouse hundreds and thousands of people to form a great force.

Yet Mao saw that if the masses were to become true agents of development, they could not be enlisted by force: "You can convince others only by reason, not by force. Force inevitably means that the one on whom it is exercised will not be convinced. Force convinces no one."

Thus, Chinese leaders, in talking with other Third World statesmen during the last few decades, have repeatedly maintained, on the basis of their own experience, that the only reasonable path the developing countries can follow is the path of socialist revolution. The emphasis here is on "socialist," that is, the revolution must be a rebellion of the people, the masses.

"Revolution," as the Chinese use the word, does not mean a total leveling of differences. As Radio Peking said in April 1972, it does not mean that all workers, peasants, and soldiers must receive the same food, wear the same clothing and the same haircut, and be photographed in identical poses. To put it briefly, a socialist revolution simply means serving the people. It represents a reversal of the old Confucianist mentality, according to which the people were the Emperor's slaves. Doing away with the hierarchy, moving from the vertical to the horizontal—that is what the revolution entails. The corollary, of course, is that everyone must take an active part in the revolution; no one may be a mere spectator. Mao explains this attitude clearly by referring to its opposite in his own youth. At that time many students were attacking the views and reactions of their elders without being clear as to their reasons. "Most of the students," Mao writes, "were on the side of rebellion, but as spectators. They did not realize that the whole business would affect their own lives. . . . I have never forgotten that."

Revolution must involve more than rebellion and revolt. It must attack the basic problem: underdevelopment and exploitation. Mao once again recalls an incident of his youth. Famine broke out in his father's district and the poor peasants attacked Mao's father, who had a grain trade. Mao opposed his father and took the side of the peasants. However, he tells us he had the feeling that the methods used by the peasants were wrong. They simply went about plundering, which did not resolve the basic problem since it did away with neither the poverty nor the exploitation of the poor.

Application to Other Developing Countries

Simple reform will never resolve the problems of development, since only what is positively related to the new can be reformed. The social structures in the developing countries are, for the most part, feudal, authoritarian, and elitist, and a whole new social order is needed. Genuine development will, therefore, be possible only by way of revolution, such as occurred in the passage from the Old Testament to the New or monarchist France to La République. Past history may contain some seeds of what is needed, but there must also be a radical breakthrough. This breakthrough need not, however, come from outside. An African or an Asian or a Latin American socialist revolution is possible.

5

THE CHARISMATIC
LEADER

Han Suyin, the well-known biographer of Mao
Tse-tung, writes in the prologue of her book *The
Morning Deluge: Mao Tse-tung and the Chinese Revolu-
tion, 1893–1954:*

The Chinese Revolution brought forth its leader in Mao
Tse-tung. Mao Tse-tung shaped the Chinese Revolution.
This dialectical link, symbiosis between a man's life and
the Revolution to which he has given his life, makes it
impossible to write of the one without the other. Mao
Tse-tung has embodied the aspirations, needs, and desires of his nation and of his people; their will to revolt, to
end exploitation, misery, injustice; to free themselves
and become masters of their own destiny. The source of
his creative power, as he will say himself, is the bound-
less creative power of the masses, who topple empires
and transform the earth. He found his own people with
limitless enthusiasm for revolution, and unhesitatingly
gave all of himself to it, and hence became their leader,
the nation-man.

Apart from Ho Chi Minh, Mao is the only Marxist leader who has come not from the city but from the land. Thus he belongs to the majority sector of the Chinese people, the peasant class to which over 70 percent of the population belongs. From the beginning he knew the problems and concerns, the sorrows and joys of the people. He never became alienated from the masses but swam always in their stream, as it were. But, in addition, he was able to put the feelings, anxieties, and needs of the people into words.

A genuine revolutionary has to be a teacher, since all events are "lessons life teaches us" and "every situation must be analyzed." Mao was trained to be a teacher, and he has remained a teacher throughout his life. At the beginning of the 1920s Mao and a friend started evening courses for illiterate laborers and artisans. For these lessons he used vocabulary with which his pupils were already familiar. Thus the first words he taught them to read and write were "work," "worker," and "exploitation." In a similar fashion he used their daily experience for his starting point in arithmetic instruction.

Mao has always been able to speak to an amazingly wide range of people and to tackle all possible questions (although his point of attack always has some connection with social, economic, and political change). He possesses a further gift—the ability to rouse many sorts of people to enthusiasm for his goals.

Mao is a practical man, concerned with the people, not with an ideology. Neither does he care about originality; he draws from the stream and throws his own contributions into it. Thus, in many instances he has simply given a Marxist or Chinese formulation to what wise men—past or present, Eastern or Western—have said and written before him.

Mao has devoted his life to the Chinese people, to the restoration of their dignity and independence. His special interest is the poorest peasants, who had the furthest to go. He likes to remind people of the old story about Yu-kung. The aged Yu-kung decided that he and his two sons would remove two large hills that blocked the road to his house. People jeered at him, saying he would never finish the task. He answered, "When I die, my sons will still be here; generation after generation will come. However high the hills are, they can grow no bigger; the shovel will make them constantly smaller. What is to keep us from leveling them?" The two mountains Mao and his people began to remove were foreign imperialism and domestic feudalism.

Westerners find it difficult to understand the ongoing dialectical relationship between Mao and his people. They accuse Mao of promoting a personal cult. And, indeed, there is no doubt that for tactical reasons Mao has kept something of the old tradition of veneration for the leader. But that veneration is directed more to his ideas than to his person. Just as the Chinese used to speak of Confucius when they actually meant his writings, so now they are actually referring to Mao Tse-tung's thoughts rather than to Mao himself.

It is an interesting fact that the Chinese really know little about Mao himself, but they can readily quote what he says. They do know about the most important phases of his life, but even these have a supra-individual significance. They are symbols, myths, and thus images to light the way for the people as a whole. Thus the conflict between Mao and Chiang Kai-shek represents the eternal conflict between revolution and reaction. The Long March—the six thousand miles the revolutionaries trod through mountains, swamps, and burning deserts into the western mountains—symbolizes the abiding destiny of a people that lives the revolution. Even the Cultural Revolution is a reminder to the people: The revolution is not something that takes place once and for all; it goes on endlessly.

Edgar Snow, who was in Yenan with Mao in 1936 and was the first Westerner to visit him when China was opened again to foreigners, spoke frequently with him about the "cult of personality." It became clear that Mao had thought a good deal about it. He knew its possible distortions and dangers, but, as an experienced popular leader, he saw that such a cult was in some degree necessary. A revolution needs a charismatic leader. "Probably Mr. Khrushchev fell because he had no cult of personality at all."

A revolution needs a pattern to follow, a point around which to crystallize, a symbol, a teacher, or a charismatic leader who serves the people. Experience has proved this to be true in the African independence movements, among others. In many developing countries today there is no strong personality who advances with the people and does not simply talk to them. But where such a personality does come to the fore, true development can be initiated. The development in Tanzania under Julius Nyerere and, despite the numerous difficulties, in its way, the development in Chile under Salvador Allende before his assassination are proofs of this.

6

THE REAL HERO
IS THE PEOPLE

Mao has always given all the credit for the revolution to the people. During the "Great Proletarian Cultural Revolution," for example, he often insisted that "the opinion of charlatans like Liu Shao-chi" that history is the work of a few geniuses is false. In Mao's view a genuine revolution has only one hero and one originator: the people.

An individual can accomplish nothing alone; even a genius can act as a genius only by standing in a positive relation to the people. The people are, in Mao's eyes, "the great wave of reality" that flows like a single stream through the whole of existence.

From the beginning of his revolutionary activity Mao has, therefore, concentrated on bringing the people to the awareness required to transform society. He has set up a dialectic, a tension between two contradictories: his faith in the omnipotence of the people (populism) and the eternal laws of historical materialism (determinism). On the one hand, he sees the total determination of human society by historical "laws of nature"; on the other, the "miracle" of a "consciousness" that moves mountains and thus shifts the "laws of nature" to a different plane. The consciousness must be strong enough to bring about both changes in society and the economic conditions required for these changes to be effective.

The revolution's first task, then, was to liberate the people. In old China, as Mao sees it, the whole feudal-patriarchal structure and ideology found its embodiment in "four powers": the religious, the political, the tribal, and, for women, the marital. With these four strong ropes the Chinese people, and especially the peasants, were kept prisoners. But even after ropes have been cut and the "liberation" accomplished Maoism still sees the important thing as the people, not the government. For example, Chou En-lai once told an American magazine:

President Nixon has listed five centers of power: the United States, the Soviet Union, China, Japan, and the European Common Market. We do not agree entirely with his view. The list may have some validity from an economic viewpoint, but not from the viewpoint of the worldwide movement of popular liberation which is the key to the future. For all nations, whatever their size, race, or color, ought to be equal. Governments find it difficult to agree with each other, but the people find it much easier to see common ground. We look to the people [*Newsweek*, February 14, 1972].

In the old China Peking was the center of things; in the new China the people are the center. Every individual is to find personal fulfillment in the people. Therefore, all Chinese are to "give themselves wholly to the service of the Chinese people." In doing this they will, in fact, be serving all the peoples of the world; in this sense the center of the world is everywhere. There is no further need of conquering the world; all that is needed is to awaken those masses who are still, in the Chinese view, being kept anesthetized by the opium of religion and of political and economic imperialism.

In 1930 Mao wrote a well-known essay, "A Single Spark Can Start a Prairie Fire." The meaning of the title is that the forces of revolution, however weak and insignificant they may be, can grow very quickly if they find the right point of insertion. In the case of China the "prairie" is the people or the peasants. Mao saw the poor peasants as the vanguard of the revolution. He wrote in 1927: "This enormous mass of poor peasants, altogether comprising 70 percent of the rural population, are the backbone of the peasant association, the vanguard in overthrowing the feudal forces, and the foremost heroes who have accomplished the great revolutionary undertaking left unaccomplished for many years."

To awaken the people is to turn them into a

creative and dynamic revolutionary force. "Every work requires a movement of the masses; without such a movement nothing is accomplished," Mao declared, and this conviction led to the creation, in the countryside and in the factories, of an atmosphere described as "ten thousand horses galloping."

Additionally, just as the Chinese revolutionaries are convinced that an individual can accomplish nothing alone, so too they believe that if individual groups splinter and allow classes to come into existence once more, nothing can be accomplished. "You cannot forge an axle with a single hammer-blow, and one pair of hands cannot establish socialism. What can I do in isolation? Let us therefore together create a new world!" (*Peking Review*, no. 30, 1973).

Thus the political mobilization of the masses, accompanied by the move toward a classless society, gave rise to a great revolutionary enthusiasm; it freed and set in motion the "powers of production." Chairman Mao can make the joyful claim: "Never has the world seen such a spiritual upsurge of the masses as today, such enthusiasm for the struggle, such ardent fervor."

In the old China the great virtue was obedience. Today (and this is constantly being drummed into the people) the great virtue is creativity—daring, inventiveness, willingness to take risks and experiment. Mao has linked his destiny with that of the workers and peasants; he has identified himself with them. Mao is not the revolution; the revolution is the people.

And in Chinese thinking the people are eternal, for Mao can die but the people live on. A single spark has indeed set the prairie on fire.

Application to Other Developing Countries

Development is something that occurs in union with the people and not simply for the people. The people must not have development thrust down their throats from above; they must first be won to the cause.

Moreover, true development is not first and foremost a matter of increasing production with the larger "pie" to be divided later on. It is first and foremost the raising of a new consciousness in the people. Only when such a consciousness is the basis for all further work can there be a development that reaches beyond economics into the political and social spheres.

7

TURNING INWARD

In the Soviet Union Lenin maintained that the industrial proletariat was an elite and should provide the leadership in the revolution, even though the larger part of the population was peasants. Mao, on the contrary, believed in the creative and revolutionary potential of the masses, who were mostly peasants. Thus, from the very beginning, Mao led China along a different path than the one followed by the Soviet Union. In the Soviet Union Lenin and his successors focused all their attention on rapid development of heavy industry; to do this they were obliged to engage in trade on a worldwide scale. Additionally, the masses (i.e., the peasants) had to be forced to supply foodstuffs to take care of the ever-growing number of workers. This meant that Russian agriculture was really "exploited" in the interests of industry.

In China the same thing happened, and is still happening, but only to a very limited extent. The first thing Mao wanted to do, indeed had to do according to his view of the revolution, was to build up the people, not industry. For to Mao, Marxism is primarily a humanistic movement, not simply a prescription for the economy. (It is in this respect that Chinese Marxism differs so radically from Soviet Marxism.)

Even with this perspective, however, Mao had to discover priorities and methods. At the beginning of the 1920s he, like the Russians before him, was still concentrating on the urban proletariat. But he soon became convinced that the entire urban phenomenon was a by-product of a society dominated almost exclusively by the profit motive. Thus it was the product of a wrong sense of direction or a one-sided mentality, in Chinese terms, the consequence of denying contraries. So the re-creation of person and society became Mao's guiding idea as he constructed a Chinese socialism.

Before the Chinese people could handle all their problems, Mao saw that they must pass through a process of purification. Those long-oppressed people had to recover their self-confidence and pride. There was no other solution than for China to shut its doors completely on the outside world. As a matter of fact, this was not too difficult in China. On the one hand, it had never been a great trading nation; on the other, it had always tended to be intellectually and economically self-supporting. (Early on, the experiment of economic relations with the Soviet Union, which was regarded as friend and ally in the international struggle for liberation, seemed an additional factor in easing the difficulties of self-containment. It soon became evident, however, that at this stage, any close economic relations, even with a "brother state," would lead to dependence and thus to colonialism.)

Liberated China thought—and still thinks—of human beings (i.e., the peasants and the workers), not raw materials, as the chief source of its wealth. The first order of business, then, was to profit by this kind of capital, but without exploiting and alienating it. The method had to be the education of the people, politically and technologically, in the crucible of revolution. The ideal of a new society truly grounded in humanism and the consequent manner of dealing with root problems became much more important to the Chinese communists than a one-sided promotion of economic growth simply for the sake of becoming a superpower as quickly as possible.

One of the revolution's first goals, therefore, was to amalgamate the peasants and workers with the civil servants, intellectuals, and students. This could be accomplished only by shifting the main focus to agriculture and the rural areas, giving the cities and foreign trade and politics only a secondary concern.

Both a cause and an effect of this shift was that the basis of development became agriculture—as it continues to be today. But for agriculture to become genuinely productive there had first to be land reform and education of the peasants. Once these programs had been accomplished, a twelve-year plan (1956–1967) for agricultural development urged the elimination of illiteracy, the construction of schools, and the strengthening of socialist awareness among the peasants. These were all steps that would enable the peasants to further help themselves while achieving progress in agriculture.

In many other developing countries such plans have been mere words. But in China they have not proved paper tigers. They have, by and large, been carried out, and not the least reason for this is that they have been realistic and changed when found not to be meeting root problems.

The First Five-Year Plan, which went into effect in 1953, had still been directed entirely toward building up the non-agricultural economy —finance, industry, transportation. Those responsible had thought that the collectivized peasants' first fervor would carry them through. But the results were meager. However, the party and its leaders were determined to learn their lesson, even from failures. The decisions they had to make were not easy, and it took many months of debate to settle the general lines of the Second Five-Year Plan. Finally, in late 1957, the Great Leap Forward began. Even then the answers to all problems had not been worked out. Only the general line of advance was clear, as the following three principles indicate:

1. Agriculture is the foundation of the economic structure, while the industry that turns out the means and

materials for production is the element that sets the whole in motion.

2. Economic development comes through the action of the masses, simultaneous development on both the large and small scale. This is a defense of a system that contains its own dynamic principle and operates in all spheres and at all levels.

3. The commune is the cell of the socialist society. (This principle was the last to be grasped and formulated.)

China's ascetical concentration on internal affairs and meeting human needs in all sectors of society has been rewarded. Today it not only has no foreign debts. Much more important, it has established a sound agricultural system that enables it, despite great climatic difficulties, to provide adequate nourishment for a quarter of the world's population—this in a country that has at its disposal barely 8 percent of the earth's cultivated area.

Application to Other Developing Countries

China, like every developing country, has made mistakes. The important thing about China is that it has continually sat in honest judgment on itself and has had the courage to draw conclusions from its errors. Certainly it is not possible for every other developing nation to turn inward as China has; for one thing most lack its size. But the choice is not usually one of either/or; rather, it is a choice of more or less. Most developing countries have depended too much on the industrialized nations and have one-sidedly limited their progress to an increase of exports and a broadening of trade. As a result, the goods they produce must relate to the demands of the world market and not to the needs of their own people. A stronger concentration on the nation itself is a prerequisite for a genuine development of the whole population.

8

THE PRIMACY
OF THE POLITICAL

Some Chinese enthusiasts wanted to make the socialist revolution an overnight reality of every aspect of life. Mao set them right in July 1955: "These comrades tackle problems in the wrong way. They concentrate not on the essential and the primary but on the accidental and the secondary. Non-essential, secondary things must of course not simply be ignored, but must be dealt with one after the other. However, they must not be thought of as essential and primary, for otherwise we will lose our bearings."

The method that Mao recommends here is the method he wants followed in assessing a situation, analyzing a problem, or arranging work: the method of setting priorities and dealing with them in due order. What are "the essential and the primary" priorities of China's revolution? One indication is the "Four Goods"—areas in which outstanding merit can win individual soldiers or whole companies a written testimonial. These "Four Goods" are 1) good political and ideological work; 2) good observance of the established rules for work; 3) good military training; 4) good organization in everyday life. Such priorities, in daily use, make it clear that the ideological takes precedence over the military, or, as Mao's instruction puts it: "Politics first in everything."

A further norm is provided by the "Four Firsts." This is another scale of values, of the kind much favored in the Confucian ethical tradition. The "Four Firsts" require that 1) in choosing between man and weapon, man comes first; 2) in choosing between political and other work, political work comes first; 3) in choosing between ideological work and other, routine political tasks, ideological work comes first; 4) in ideological work, ideas directly connected with life come before academic wisdom.

Therefore, the following is the true order of values: 1) man; 2) political work; 3) ideological work; 4) ideas based on life.

In China the meaning of "politics" is simple and clear: relationship to the people. The "primacy of the political" means, concretely, the thought of Mao Tse-tung, and this in turn means the life and existence of the people finding expression in idea, word, and action. "If we are properly to grasp the essential and most important aspect of things, we must firmly maintain the proletarian viewpoint," said Mao in his 1955 speech, and he added, "Our viewpoint is that of the proletariat and the broad masses of the people." This is Maoism's basic point of departure for setting priorities, for approaching any problem. According to the Chinese revolutionaries, anyone who adopts the viewpoint of the individual or of a limited group instead of the proletariat will certainly make a false assessment of the situation and fail to analyze properly the contradictions it brings into play.

The primacy of the political holds in every area and has many ramifications. For example, giving the political priority over the military means that the soldier remains first and foremost a member of the people; consequently, the military cannot gradually develop into a clique or new caste. Another example: During the Cultural Revolution Mao said with regard to technology and the economy, "To be red [i.e., in solidarity with the proletariat] is of far greater value than to be an expert."

The "primacy of the political" means also that it was tackled first in time. The former president of the National Academy of Fine Arts explained to an American art journal why the ancient tradition could not be emphasized and fostered in the early years of the revolution: "Political work had to come first. The popular revolution had to be carried through; a new consciousness and a new way of thinking had to be formed, promoted, and put into practice."

Liu Shao-chi and his allies were, therefore, called traitors because they tried to make the economy more important than man, sought to increase production without a class struggle, promoted effective work by promising material rewards rather than by applying ideological stimuli, and stood for the priority of the economic over the political, in the service of technology. Mao complained to Edgar Snow that these people would have preferred an extension of public credit to "great leaps forward," and thereby manifested a politically motivated faith in capital.

In practice the primacy of the political means simply that the interests of the whole country must take precedence over secondary or individual interests. Charles Bettelheim, professor at the École Pratique des Hautes Études in Paris and Director of the Study Center for Socialist Planning comments:

Here we have the driving force behind an economic progress of a new kind, a progress connected with the fact that production is no longer controlled by the effort at a higher exchange value or a higher profit or an increased cash flow, but by the quest for greater usefulness.

This represents a radical change in social relations as regards both the economic basis and the superstructure.

Application to Other Developing Countries

In the Chinese tradition (as well as in the Western, Aristotelian tradition) politics means "having to do with the people." If this definition is accepted then development must be a political matter. Only concentration on the whole people, the common good, can give development a humanistic direction. This direction, as the Chinese experience shows, will then be a condition for and source of new forms of developing the economy. If, on the other hand, one starts with the economic and avoids the political (or simply fails to take it into account), one will end up with nothing but "white elephants." If one seeks to develop *only* technological resources or *only* means of economic progress, one will have excluded from one's purview the totality, the political—in other words, the people.

9

THE ARMY
IS THE PEOPLE

In the summer of 1972, the Chinese People's Liberation Army (PLA) celebrated the forty-fifth anniversary of its formation by Mao Tse-tung. On this occasion he emphasized a point he has never tired of repeating: that the chief task of the PLA is political. The primary purpose of the army is not to crush foreign enemies but to foster unity with the people. "Political work is its central concern."

Mao has lived by a tradition which his army understands: "The sword may win, but only the *logos* ["the word," "wisdom"] can preserve." Or, in the words that Chinese tradition says a sage addressed to the first emperor of the Han dynasty: "You have conquered a kingdom from the saddle, but you cannot rule it from the saddle."

Not only has Mao made this wisdom his guide. He has also extended it even more radically. The soldier must alight from the saddle to such an extent that he need never climb back into it. The goal of the PLA is to bring the new society into existence; that is what its "political work" means. At a later stage there will be no strictly military tasks left. In the new socialist society of China, there will be no distinction between soldier, farmer, worker, official, or party member. Already the people are the army and the army is the people. Another way of expressing this same viewpoint is to say that the PLA is "the school of the nation" or of the revolution. Because the army will eventually meld completely into the general population, stress has been laid on its civil functions from the beginning. As far back as the 1930s, in Kiangsi and Yenan, the PLA not only had the job of protecting and fighting for the people; it also played a decisive role in educating and organizing the people. By 1949, after the revolution had been victorious, Mao could say: "The army is a school. Our army of 2,100,000 in the field is worth many thousand universities and secondary schools." And, more recently, Premier Chou En-lai explained, "The army unites us all." The "Great Three" —people, army, and party—are being fused together and depend upon each other, as the Chinese would put it, "like lips and teeth."

In its political, civil functions, the PLA is involved with farming and industrial production, for itself and for educational purposes. Each division is independent when it comes to providing itself with food and with certain products, such as shoes, clothing, and machinery. This is why Chinese military posts are located amid farmland and look like communes. Agricultural machinery stands alongside cannons. Many military bases have no surrounding fences or "keep out" signs. In short, there are no dividing lines between the military and the rest of the people. Rather, the army has become a model and school for the people by giving an example of how to plant, harvest, drain swamps, and build bridges and roads. To some extent it even performs administrative tasks. Indeed its political and social functions are regarded as more important than its strictly military ones. Mao can therefore say, "Our troops dedicate themselves completely to the liberation of the people and are wholly at the service of the people's interests." And the former Defense Minister Lin Piao stated, "The people must learn from the army."

In addition, since the beginning of 1927 Mao has carried on a campaign against an elitist mentality in the military. Until 1949 there was even no distinction between civil and military personnel in the PLA. His constant effort has been to democratize the army; there are no signs of rank, no wearing of medals, and people cannot tell a commander from a factory worker. Tasks are assigned according to need and talent, resulting in the phenomenon of officers with temporary commissions.

The PLA has not kept its proletarian character without many struggles. Many in the military have not understood what Mao is after; they have tried to cut themselves off from the people, lead a special existence of their own, and depend more on weapons (especially atom bombs) than on people. Shortly after the victory of 1949 the army began to become independent. The elitist, sectarian tendency of the military began to manifest itself; militarism, bureaucratism, and authoritarianism came on the scene again. One purpose of the Cultural Revolution was to relieve this situation.

Today there are signs that a similar revisionist spirit is springing up. Even Lin Piao, after his enthusiasm for the Cultural Revolution, has become a victim of the trend. But his successor, Marshal Yeh Chien-ying, though already 75 years old, seems to possess the new spirit. For example, at his installation he appeared in civilian dress, and, in the best dialectical tradition, turned Lin Piao's statement around: "The army must learn from the people."

Over the past forty-five years the PLA has managed to draw the people in its wake and has thus given an immense impetus to development. It represents an important link to the life of the masses and seeks to integrate itself with them through its work of organization, propaganda, production, and services.

The integration has been effected to such an extent that the impression is sometimes given that "everyone is a soldier." In that sense China has been militarized—a disquieting thought for many. It is evidently not easy to apply Western statistical methods to this kind of army. According to Chinese sources "hundreds of millions of men and women" belong to the army. The London Institute for Strategic Studies regards that figure as the rhetoric of propaganda and has estimated that the effective strength could hardly be more than five million. But it was precisely this kind of "calculation" that proved fatal to the United States in Vietnam. What makes the Chinese army unique and highly interesting is the manner in which it is used: to serve the people.

Application to Other Developing Countries

In a growing number of developing countries the army has taken control. But these armies are states within the state. The officers have not passed through the school of the people but through the military academies at West Point, Sandhurst, or Saint-Cyr, where they were Westernized, alienated, militarized, and educated to be an isolated elite. As a result, these men, though perhaps few in numbers, are already much stronger than any political movement still in its infancy and are, therefore, easily tempted to take over political as well as military power. If they are at all interested in development, they think as technocrats and are thus automatically dependent on their earlier "masters" in the United States, France, or England. And so the vicious circle closes once again.

The example of China shows that the army can play an immensely important role in development, but to do so it must emerge from and return to the people. It must take to heart the ancient peasant wisdom that growth can never be achieved by muscle, that after preparing the fields the farmer must wait patiently for the harvest. Applied to development, this means the military *per se* must take second place; the first place belongs to the arts of persuasion, to the raising of the masses' consciousness, and to politics. In China the PLA is not a professional elite set apart from the people to live unproductively while eating up the people's taxes. It is one with the people and leads them along the path of development.

10

CONTRARIES IN THOUGHT AND ACTION

A long tradition of dialectic—thinking in contraries—has kept China from going to extremes.

"Contrariety" in Chinese is *mao-tun*. The two syllables mean "lance" and "shield," representing an existential conflict of opponents, such as "forward and backward," "hither and thither," "strength and weakness." The lance pierces the shield, and the shield turns the lance aside; the one negates the other, and the conflict is underway.

A sensitivity to sharp antitheses is deeply rooted in the Chinese mentality and reflected in its language and history, as has been pointed out by scholars such as Wolfgang Bauer, Joachim Schickel, and Hans Heinz Holz.

The Taoist wisdom of ancient China particularly

emphasizes antitheses; much of its tradition consists in maintaining a "both/and" rather than an "either/or." The great Taoist teacher, Lao-Tzu, said: "Being and non-being beget each other; heavy and light perfect each other; long and short shape each other; high and low subvert each other. . . ; before and after follow upon one another."

In speaking of dialectic, Mao has repeatedly invoked the Taoist tradition. Indeed, Bauer is of the opinion that the strategic and tactical principles of guerrilla warfare, as developed by Mao, are based on Taoist dialectic.

This thinking in contraries emerges with special clarity in Mao's sixteen-point formula for partisan warfare. There he says: "The enemy advances, we retreat. The enemy halts, we harass. The enemy withdraws, we attack. The enemy retreats, we pursue."

Another statement of Mao's involving dialectic explains how comprehensive a military (or any operation) must be, since it must take both poles into account:

The only statement that is entirely correct is: that a revolution or revolutionary war is an offensive yet has also its defensive phase and retreat. To defend in order to attack, to retreat in order to advance, to take a flanking position in order to take a frontal action, and to be devious in order to go direct—these are inevitable occurrences in the process of development of many things, and military movements cannot be otherwise.

Mao has even written an essay titled "On Contradiction." It discusses how properly to handle the contraries found in the people. In it he says:

There is nothing that does not contain contradiction; without contradiction there would be no world. . . .

If in the Party there were neither contradictions nor ideological struggles to solve them, the Party's life would come to an end. . . .

A contradictory aspect cannot exist in isolation. Without the other aspect which is opposed to it, each aspect loses the condition of its existence. . . .

Without life, there would be no death; without death, there would also be no life. Without "above," there would be no "below"; without "below," there would also be no "above." Without misfortune, there would be no good fortune; without good fortune, there would also be no misfortune. Without facility, there would be no difficulty; without difficulty, there would also be no facility. Without landlords, there would be no tenant-peasants; without tenant-peasants, there would also be no landlords. Without the bourgeoisie, there would be no proletariat; without a proletariat, there would also be no bourgeoisie.

These few examples—which could be expanded if room permitted—give some idea of the extent to which the dialectic of "both/and" permeates Mao Tse-tung's thinking; the opposite side of any situation is always taken into account, even if it is not expressed in so many words. Consequently, there is a much greater grasp of totality than in the West, and the thinking is more honest, realistic, pragmatic, and human.

At first thought, the Western mind often finds this creative acceptance of antitheses difficult and exceedingly philosophic. However, as we now see in China, it can have very practical applications. For example, since Chinese thought always takes the other side of things into account, it does not tend to slip into one-sided, unhealthy kinds of development as easily as the West does. Praxis is included and preserved in theory: the countryside in the city, bodily work in mental, light industry in heavy, the circumference in the center, the expert in the layperson, the young in the old, the word in the sword, the woman in the man, the minority in the majority, the individual in the people.

Thus Maoism, like all Marxist political thought, follows the ins and outs of any given subject, including its inherent contradictions. But the Chinese mind goes one step further to a logical conclusion: Following these ins and outs the political thought will itself fall into defect and error and, therefore, need continual correction. Thus, Maoism is not nearly as dogmatic as the West may think it to be. Quite unlike the Soviet version of Marxism, Maoist Marxism includes criticism as an essential principle of the dialectic which is grasped by the mind.

For example, the struggle with the dialectic of old and new leaves open the possibility that the new may be worse than the old. So the Chinese see clearly that the possibility of retrogression is built into the very system. But, as Mao puts it: "Without contradiction there would be no world," and "one must go backwards in order to advance."

Thinking in this way, Mao and his colleagues have been able to advance and to yield as needed. They have known from the beginning that the right will be (or may be) succeeded by the wrong. Therefore, they have always been aware that they must take a critical stance in order to preserve the totality, the unity, the tension between the poles.

Of course, this attitude has presented Mao with continual difficulties from the radical left, which would prefer to proceed in a dogmatic way. But Mao answers: "Classes and the class struggle continue to be part of a transitional society." He says that it is possible to deal with this contradiction only through struggle, criticism, and reorganization along the path traced by the Great Proletarian Cultural Revolution. For Mao and his followers "we must constantly create the revolution, change things, criticize, search out our own weaknesses, and correct them."

Such an approach gives Chinese thought and action a great mobility and creativeness in dealing with everyday life; it also helps people put up with failures. For an outsider, however, the language of dialectic is hard to understand at times.

Take, for example, an incident during the Tenth Congress of the Chinese Communist Party, in August 1973. Wang Hung-wen, third man in the Party hierarchy (after Mao Tse-tung and Chou En-lai) quoted a well-known statement of Mao that was also incorporated in the New Constitution of the Party. However, he omitted from the statement some words hitherto regarded as very important: "The individual must subordinate himself to the organization, and the minority to the majority." In the language of Chinese dialectic, Wang was saying something without stating it explicitly, namely, that at the present juncture in resolving contradictions greater emphasis is needed on the individual and the minorities.

At the same Congress Chou En-lai said that a true Communist must be ready to accept high and low positions alike and be capable of ascending and descending the ladder repeatedly over the course of his life. That is the dialectic as concretely lived, and it gives the whole system a high degree of flexibility and mobility.

Such dynamic, tension-filled thinking has made it possible for the Chinese to resolve contradictions which the West regards as fixed and irreducible. This is especially true of the contraries that are so important in the development process: theory and practice, industry and agriculture, urban and rural areas, mental and physical work, even unity and criticism.

In the Chinese experiment these contradictions are, in fact, present, but they are resolved in a creative way. For example, there continue to be distinctions among various tasks, but there is an elimination of distinctions among the people assigned to them. Through the resolution and

unification of such contradictions, a greater whole-
ness, and with it a greater equality, have come to
mark Chinese society.

The dialectic has also made possible what the
Chinese call "walking on both legs." Liu Shao-chi
explains this phrase:

The simultaneous development of industry and agriculture, and of heavy industry and light industry, with
heavy industry being given greater importance; the
simultaneous development of centrally and locally ad-
ministered individual works, and of large, medium, and
small enterprises; and the simultaneous use of modern
and more traditional methods of production, under cen-
tralized guidance and under a comprehensive plan.

This whole series of measures was later called by the
people "walking on both legs" [see Chapter 17 below for a
discussion of the application of this principle].

Application to Other Developing Countries

Most of the developing countries are in great
danger because they subscribe to a single theory.
Too often they take over the "either/or" thinking of
the West, and the result is an easy slide into dogmatism and absolutism. There is also the danger of
ideologism. Their development is then one-sided
and affects only certain strata of the society. In
addition, many of their governments are far too
proud and sensitive to correct their defects because
acceptance of the possibility of making mistakes is
not built into the system; consequently any criti-

cism is immediately an attack on the leadership.

Thinking according to the dialectical method —not denying contradictions but seeking to unite them—would be far more human and social and, in the last analysis, of far greater service to all. For, as the Chinese model shows us, dialectical thinking preserves a sense of the whole. Additionally, making explicit place for the possibility of mistakes inculcates a measure of patience, as well as allowing for their discovery and criticism. Development then becomes an ongoing, always vital process.

11

THE IMPORTANCE
AND DANGER
OF CADRES

In Mao's view, the revolution must have a strong
Party organization, as well as a solid basis in the
masses and a popular army of liberation. He explained in 1937:

The organization of our Party must be expanded
throughout the country; it must purposefully train tens of
thousands of cadres and several hundreds of excellent
mass leaders. These cadres and leaders . . . must have
political insight and ability to work, they must be full of
the spirit of self-sacrifice, capable of solving problems
independently; and they must remain firm in the midst of
difficulties and work loyally and devotedly for the nation,
the class and the Party. Only through these people can
the Party be linked with its membership and the masses,
and only through the firm leadership these people give to
the masses can the Party succeed in defeating the enemy.
    These people must not be tainted with selfishness,

individual heroism or vain gloriousness, indolence or passivity, or arrogant sectarianism; they must be selfless heroes of the nation and the class.

In the following year, he again stated:

Once the correct political line has been determined, the cadres will become the decisive factor. Hence to rear large numbers of new cadres according to plan is our fighting task [from "The Role of the Chinese Communist Party in the National War, 1938"].

The members of the Party are, for Mao, to be like seed growing in the soil of the people. Wherever the members find themselves, they are to identify themselves with the people, take root in them, and bear fruit in their midst. They "must be men of wide vision, be self-sacrificing in a supreme degree, show the highest honesty, and be able to grasp a situation with complete openness of mind."

This principle continues strong today. The first chapter of the new Communist Party Constitution, adopted August 28, 1973, at the Tenth Congress of the Chinese Communist Party, states:

The Party must find its support in the working class, strengthen the unity of workers and peasants, and give leadership to the masses of people of all nationalities who make up the nation. It must moreover help to develop the three great revolutionary movements—the class struggle, the effort at production, and scientific experimentation—and do so in an independent and self-sufficient way, with trust in its own strength, through a difficult struggle, with diligence and thrift, with the use of all its

65

powers, always striving to build more quickly a better, more extensive, and more economically stable socialism, to prepare for possible war and natural catastrophes, and to do all this for the people.

In other words, without the masses there is no revolution, but without dedicated Party leaders and cadres, the masses will not be set in motion.

The Chinese Communist Party, with this as its dominant spirit, is already part of history. It is the Party with the longest experience and training in the political and military struggle. Early on, its founders were forced to separate themselves from the people and join the Red Army on the Long March of 1934 into the mountains of Yenan. Work with the people was then taken up all the more energetically during the advance of the Red Army against the forces of Chiang Kai-shek.

The Chinese Communist Party found itself and developed through the struggle against the opportunism of the right and the left. All members of the Party must be filled with the revolutionary spirit; they must have courage to swim against the stream, and must hold fast to the principles of Marxism, not of revisionism. They must be open and honest and not engage in conspiracies or underhanded trickery; they must be able to distinguish and deal with the various contradictions between us and the enemy as well as those to be found among the people; they must develop a style of work that is characterized by the union of theory and practice, close association with the masses, and criticism, including self-criticism. They must train up millions who will carry on the revolutionary cause of the proletariat [New Party Constitution, 1973].

Continual Purification of the Party

The Communists are in charge of the revolution because, in the Party itself and in the army, they have created institutions, convictions, and hopes which have enabled the leadership and the cadres to draw the rural masses after them. This is the role Mao believes they should continue to play.

Human nature being what it is, however, individuals and groups can lose sight of this role. After the revolution had been won, some Party officials succumbed to bureaucratism and dogmatism. Yet so numerous were the reserves at the Party's disposition that in the Cultural Revolution of 1966 it became the first Communist Party in history that deliberately roused the masses against itself. This about-turn was called the *Cultural* Revolution because its first blow was directed against the Party's propaganda bosses, who were said to have taken a bourgeois and capitalist line in the cultural area. It is interesting to note that the new Constitution accepts the necessity of such cultural revolutions as inevitable: "Revolutions of this kind will be repeated in the future."

Thus, we can see that the Chinese are well aware that the Party cadre brings with it the danger of a new elite or a new class. The attractions of exclusivity are always waiting to lay hold of the people. For this reason Mao has increasingly inclined to the idea that Party officials should also share in the collective work of production so that their links with the people may be closer. Leaders and cadre members must be proletarian politicians who are able to join the vast majority of people in the common toil. "They are not to seek out only those who think as they do, but must be able to join hands with those of differing views and even with those who had taken the lists against them" (Mao).

Within the Party the committee system plays an important part. There Party members learn to reach collective decisions and to engage in collective work. Then they go out to become group leaders among the people. In view of this and in view of the fact that one of the five conditions of Party membership is the "courage to engage in criticism, even self-criticism," the slogan that "the Party directs everything" acquires a somewhat different meaning than it has in the West.

The Party and its members have as their task making Mao's thought the norm everywhere and on all occasions. This is partially accomplished by exercising a constant critique and creating an environment of reminders. As one Chinese explained to a Western visitor: "Is it wrong for us to wash our brains now and then, since, after all, we wash our bodies, don't we?"

This critique by the Party and its cadres gives a new direction to people's thinking. It is done in the service of the people, so as to educate them and ultimately to convert them. The emblems, symbols, streamers, slogans, radios, and loudspeakers that are to be found everywhere and that Westerners see merely as a vast propaganda program have the same kind of meaning that churches, wayside crosses, wooden poles bearing holy images, medals, and relics had for Christendom during the Middle Ages. To the faithful they are not a burden but the expression of a new awareness.

Application to Other Developing Countries

Between the charismatic leader or the government and the people there has to be a mediating task force. This is the Party or the cadres. Such a linking agent is absolutely necessary, but there is a danger, as the Chinese experience, among others, has shown, that officials or cadres may someday turn into a new elite, a privileged class of bureaucrats. Therefore the system ought to make it possible, as it does in China, to restore the Party and the cadres to their original purpose through an internally directed revolution whenever necessary. The one-party system that operates in many developing countries is often misunderstood: It can indeed be the moving force behind development, provided that the party contains all the contraries within itself, knows how to deal with them, and remains in close contact with the people.

12

TRUST IN YOUR OWN STRENGTH

In 1973, Wang Yua-yi, the Chinese representative to the United Nations Industrial Development Association (UNIDA) meeting in Vienna, attempted to explain the Chinese model of development to the rest of the world. He began by admitting that China, too, wants and needs industrialization:

It is the general desire of peoples in the developing countries to develop their own industry and to see their countries industrialized. For, as we all know, without industry there can be no economic independence; the people cannot achieve prosperity nor can the State flourish and be strong.

The key word is "independence." Industrialization must not lead to new and worse forms of dependency than existed before political independence was won.

In this area China has been able to learn much

from its own historical experience. Wang referred to this lesson:

In the dark days of the old China they tried to follow the path of "rescuing the country through industrialization." They thought they could develop industry on a national scale and find a way for the State to develop independently, simply by getting investment loans, machinery, and scientific and technological know-how from abroad. Despite their intense efforts, however, China became poorer and weaker. It continued to experience foreign oppression and intimidation.

The Chinese managed to escape the threat of new dependencies by turning inward, but that move was possible only because they trusted in their own strength. Wang explained this principle very specifically:

Trusting in your own strength means that a country takes its concrete condition as its starting point and, relying on the strength and wisdom of its people, gradually moves, in a carefully prepared and planned way, to eliminate the influence of imperialistic forces. It gains control of its own economic lifelines, develops its natural resources, and builds up an agriculture and a light and heavy industry that answer to the needs of its own people.

As is typical in Chinese thought, the movement included establishing a "right relationship" between contraries: between agriculture and industry both heavy and light, between domestic and foreign, between upper and lower levels, between centralization and decentralization, between city and countryside, and so forth. The proper handling of these relationships proved to be the key to rapid development. A first principle of these relationships was "to consider agriculture as the foundation and industry as the leading factor." A second principle: "We encourage confidence in our own strength; we hope for help from abroad but cannot allow ourselves to depend on it. We rely on our own efforts and the creative powers of the army and the entire people."

At the UNIDA meeting Wang elaborated on these priorities:

The struggles which the developing countries experience show that trust in one's own strength is the *most important thing* and that international help based on equal rights and mutual profit must be *secondary*, if the path to the development of national industry and to industrialization is to be reliable and trustworthy.

Mao had set the course of China trusting in its own strength as early as 1945. After victory in the war of resistance against the Japanese invaders, he said: "On what basis should our policy rest? It should rest on our own strength, and that means regeneration through one's own efforts. We are not alone; all the countries and peoples in the world opposed to imperialism are our friends. Nevertheless, we stress regeneration through our own efforts." Throughout the years since, he has frequently repeated this exhortation, elaborating it in words and even more in the actions to which he has led his people.

This course of self-trust has had very wide ramifications for the Chinese people—psychological as well as practical. Trust in one's own strength means productivity from one's strength. Self-confidence arises only out of personal experience. Only actual participation in the struggle can give rise to the revolutionary spirit and thus to self-confidence.

It took an enormously intense psychological motivation to produce the Chinese miracle. That motivation took the form of self-confidence—which itself arose out of experience. No group achieves self-confidence and pride if its work is done by others. Gifts or help can be a source of shame and forced gratitude; they can make the recipients helpless and powerless. People gain self-confidence only when they share understanding and decisions, when they travel the road together, when they share experiences and sufferings. Now that the Chinese have gained this self-confidence they have been able to adopt a motto, not of obedience and servility (as understood before the revolution), but of initiative and experiment in the socialist spirit.

This spirit made possible the gigantic step forward "from feudal obedience to scientific thinking." Responsibility for oneself has created a new morality. Work has ceased to be simply a way of earning a living and has become almost a religious experiment.

All visitors to China are impressed by the people's spartan way of life and the hard physical labor they do. These have also come from trusting in one's own strength, because that means moderating one's claim and being satisfied with what one has. The result is both great contentment and great thrift. The Chinese accept their kind of life as self-evident, but it is also a source of pride to them. They do not look on their hard lot as something forced upon them or as a form of wretchedness. Rather, by way of the self-denial and sacrifice that have been required of them, they have won through to meaning and creativity.

Trust in one's own strength has also brought into play a unique spirit of inventiveness. In order to achieve self-sufficiency it was necessary not to imitate but to create, for imitation leads to dependency while inventiveness and creativity lead to freedom. The words "study and experiment" are now part of the peasants' daily vocabulary, the idea of research is familiar to them. Because this new consciousness is everywhere, China has an inexhaustible potential at its disposal. Everything seems possible because China has secured a permanent, almost limitless reserve by managing to mobilize, transform, modernize, and inspire its base: the masses. The process of development has not been the work simply of a small elite; rather it has gone on everywhere, a decentralized, widespread process involving the whole people. Through applying the concept of "trust in your own strength," China has set in motion a landslide that has reshaped the earth.

Han Suyin gives concrete examples of these changes. In 1967 she wrote:

China can itself produce 90 percent of the equipment and machinery it needs. Steel production increased from 75 to 90 percent of total need during the period 1958–1965. Diversification and decentralization of industry have enabled every province and autonomous region in the country to develop a rather modern industry. In the short space of a dozen years the basis for a socialist industrialization was established [*China in the Year 2001*, p. 86].

Thus trust in one's own strength has, in practice, led to self-sufficiency. Today the Chinese have enough to eat, have no trouble getting adequate clothing, have suitable housing, and are so united and organized that no individual ever again need fear being shoved into a marginal existence.

It is interesting to note that the idea of self-reliance applies to the communes, too. Every commune is proud of living up to the "Three Thou Shalt Nots":

Ask no money from the government, not even loans for projects; do it yourselves!

Ask no help from another commune, not even in the form of workers; try to deal with your own situation.

Do not become discouraged by any difficulty, however great, nor even by the laws of nature; change the sun, the moon and the stars, and the whole world!

Application to Other Developing Countries

Through colonialism and the resultant continuing political, economic, and social dependence, most developing countries have lost their self-reliance. True self-confidence cannot be regained through help from outside; rather the people must first restore their own pride. As the Chinese model shows, trust in one's own strength is the most important thing; international aid is secondary, even when that can be accepted on the basis of equal rights and mutual profit. International help, like any other, is truly helpful only when it is a help to self-help.

Self-reliance, self-responsibility, self-initiative, and self-denial must become key words in any modern theory of development. Only thus can a people gain control of their own destiny.

13

NATURE ITSELF MUST BE CHANGED

"If you've got two hands, you can do anything!"
The new principle of self-sufficiency and trusting in
one's own strength has radically changed the
Chinese worldview. Old China could not conceive
of making nature subservient to man; such a notion
would have been considered presumptuous as well
as impossible. Confidence that the very heavens
could be conquered would have been regarded as
blasphemous arrogance.

The people thought of themselves as helpless in
the face of their country's physical nature, especially its mighty rivers and unpropitious climate.
They came to terms with nature and never thought
of fighting back against the injuries it did them. As a
result, the Chinese had developed not into a firmly
rooted oak but a rice field that bends before the
storm. Further, the existence of the individual, who

is mortal and subject to whims of nature, came to be regarded as of little consequence; importance could be given only to the clan, which was, for practical purposes, immortal.

The Chinese revolution brought a change. It attacked and, in large measure, rooted out this attitude of fatalism. Nature and its uncontrollable factors are still there, but they do not affect the course of development, for the people have taken their destiny into their own hands. The new person of China acts in the belief that, together with others, one can change natural laws, even guide the course of sun and moon. The Chinese of today trust in their own abilities; they are self-reliant without being arrogant; they are convinced that together they can solve all problems.

Chinese newspapers and periodicals are constantly reporting the victories of people over unruly nature. Until China was reopened to the outside world the West derided these reports as fictions. But now eyewitnesses testify they are not baseless exercises in propaganda, but narrations of things that have actually happened. In them, facts are offered as examples, intended to encourage other communes or areas of China. The newspaper reports are like the scriptural account of Jesus' miracles; they tell about events that have actually happened and are offered as proof to the Chinese that their faith is true.

Recently, many of these stories have dealt with

agricultural achievements in 1972. After ten successive years of good weather and rich harvests, in that year China had to cope with an exceptionally severe drought and other adverse natural conditions. Yet, according to various reports, the harvest was as good as in 1970. This, of course, encouraged farmers all over the country to push onward to complete irrigation systems and other modernization schemes. The existence of these will, in turn, increase the farmers' ability to overcome the opposition of nature.

For example, in one report the elderly Wang Shan-chiu, formerly a poor peasant, relates:

In 1925 the drought lasted forty-two days and the seed withered. Except for the family of a property-owner the other nineteen families in our village had to take up begging. Last year (1972) the drought lasted one hundred and eight days, yet the yield in grain and cotton was greater than in 1971. No one lacked for food or clothing. In fact, when the proceeds were divided at the end of the year, we even received some cash [*Peking Review*, no. 24, 1973].

Another case of overcoming the effects of the 1972 drought was reported from the area of Hsiyang in the province of Shansi. Even in the previous year there had been insufficient rain; then during the first five months of 1972 it did not snow or rain at all. The five rivers of the area dried up, and so did most of the reservoirs. Eighty percent of the acreage was so parched that neither ploughing nor sowing was possible. Yet the peasants of the Hsiyang area were not stymied by this catastrophic situation.

They carried a step further the revolutionary spirit of Tachai [the model agricultural village] by bringing water on carrying poles or in carts or jugs so that the over thirty-six thousand acres of farmland in the area could be ready for sowing at the proper time. Another miracle was performed, as the masses of peasants conquered nature [*Peking Review*, no. 32, 1973].

The report continues by explaining that in this area preparing a single *mu* of land (about one-thirty-seventh of an acre) usually required a hundred carrying-poles of water transported by hand over 1000 *li* (about 303 miles). For this reason the popular saying was: "1000 *li*, 100 carrying-poles, 1 *mu* freshly sown." All 80,000 members of the commune—not just the 50,000 assigned to work in the fields—took part in the water transport project; even the cadre played a heroic part. Water was something precious, as was the material victory over the drought, but most precious of all was the demonstration of "the revolutionary spirit for the building of socialism."

The impact of these accounts is difficult for a Westerner to imagine. In the 1930s John L. Buck conducted an extensive study of Chinese agriculture. He concluded that each older person had experienced, on the average, three famines in his lifetime. During them, about 8 percent of the affected population in the grain-growing regions would die of hunger and 90 percent would have to leave the area. Every one of the survivors still remembers these famines. Consider, then, their enthusiasm for a changed society which can fight nature and win.

No wonder then that since the revolution, especially since the Great Leap Forward and the Cultural Revolution, the Chinese have shown an extraordinary enthusiasm for building irrigation systems and taking steps to combat erosion. In the lowlands, many measures have been taken to offset flooding. River beds have been dredged, new river mouths have been dug, levees have been heightened and strengthened, and along the rivers reservoirs have been built to take the overflow. Amid earthquakes whose extent staggers the imagination, and with the help of nothing but carrying-poles and baskets, the agricultural communes have leveled countless terraces out of the loess and shaped them into shallow saucers by heightening the rims. Then, at the lowest point of these saucer-shaped terraces, they have dug cisterns several yards deep, so that there is always water for irrigation.

Every year since the liberation, during the winter and early spring, when not much agricultural work can be done, more than ten million peasants have engaged in building irrigation systems alone. It is reported that during the winter of 1956/57, about one hundred million peasants throughout the country were occupied in building various kinds of waterworks. In the winter of 1972/73, work was done on 1,130,000 projects, including reservoirs, dikes, dams, sluices, wells, canals, and pump stations; the result was the addition or improvement of 7,558,200 acres of irrigated land added or improved. In addition, 32,925,100 acres were leveled and deep-ploughed. Extensive sections of slope were terraced, a great deal of salty soil was improved, and 210,000 new wells were dug.

Equally impressive are the afforestation projects, so necessary to combat erosion. In the winter of 1956/57 alone over fourteen million acres of trees were planted.

It is difficult to comprehend the achievements of the Chinese people. Between 1949 and 1960 about 508 million cubic feet of dirt were shifted—that is the equivalent of digging 960 Suez Canals! Without exaggeration, then, it can be said that the power of the people is conquering nature.

Application to Other Developing Countries

By an immense effort the Chinese are increasingly freeing themselves from fatalistic dependence on their climate and on nature generally. Today, drought and famine in India and the Sahel, as well as in many other areas of the Third World, are slowly forcing people to discover what the Chinese have been learning since the liberation: Nature can be subordinated and conquered by the collective efforts of human beings.

Because of this, both have and have-not nations must come to see that the work of development cannot be accomplished through supplements or gifts from outside. It requires a change in human beings, and through them, in nature; it requires a new attitude to the world. Nature can be brought into the service of the people. This really radical challenge can be best expressed by saying: "Society takes priority over nature; nature does not have the final say." Development, therefore, requires a conversion from passivity and the fatalistic acceptance of natural phenomena to activity and the creative transformation of nature.

14

LIBERATION IN THE COMMUNE

According to China expert Joachim Schickel, Chinese thinking, "whenever given responsible expression, has been socially oriented thinking." For the Chinese mentality the Great Society is simply a restatement of a very ancient concept, since the individual Chinese has always felt himself to be part of a larger whole. Today this larger whole is most immediately the commune and then the state. In the communes the contraries—old and young, man and woman, work and school, etc.—are brought into unity, women as well as men, families as well as individuals, are liberated and brought into society. The communes have given the Chinese a sense of community and a sense of sharing in the total enterprise and thus in controlling events; this, in turn, has led to incredible feats of self-sacrifice on behalf of the nation.

English economist Joan Robinson has described a commune as "a microcosmic people's economy." It is a practical way of gaining rational control over an immense country. Because it embraces not only agriculture but local industry, trade, education, and the administration of law, it is a "small people's economy" within the overall economy. A commune is thus in great measure self-sufficient. Sputnik, the first people's commune (in Honan province), defined itself in the first article of its constitution:

The people's commune is to be a basic social institution which the working population freely forms under the leadership of the Chinese Communist Party and the people's regime, and which, in its own geographical area, takes upon itself the whole work of industrial and agricultural production, distribution, cultural and educational undertakings, and political affairs.

Immediately after the revolution the arable land had been divided among the peasants, not according to a commune system, but in the fashion of a liberal land reform. However, the Chinese leaders quickly saw that their simple redistribution of land was soon going to create rich and poor peasants again—partly because individual peasants differ so widely in abilities, even more because there are so many variables before which the individual is helpless: climate, quality of the soil, water supply, and so on. The high leadership realized that "only by means of constant social development can China

85

resolve the contradictions that affect it, and establish its position at home and abroad." By the end of 1957 they decided to apply radically new methods to the backward rural areas; these were summed up in the Great Leap Forward and the establishment of the people's communes. The Great Leap called for universal mobilization of energies; in the rural sectors this meant the planned, coordinated use of all sources of human effort and other growth factors, in an effort that could transcend the narrow limits of the Rural Productivity Associations (RPAs). To this end, people's communes were established in various places during 1958, and the system was soon extended to the whole country.

It is important to note that collectivization took place gradually in China. First, the rural areas were organized by simple mutual assistance teams, then by lower level RPAs, then higher level RPAs. The final step of forming the communes was not taken until each of these progressively more collectivized stages had been achieved. Thus the people were prepared for the development of true communes. From the 1949 slogan "A field for every farmer" to the 24,000 communes formed in 1958 (out of the 740,000 RPAs) was a far cry, but the people had been educated to see that local self-sufficiency would never be achieved without collectivization.

By 1972 there were about 74,000 people's communes in China. Each is a large community of families, numbering from a few hundred to over ten thousand, and usually located in many villages.

Most of the communes are divided into brigades, the brigades into teams, and the teams into work squads. A brigade contains, on the average, about 200 households and has its own elementary schools and small industries. The team, with anywhere from twenty to forty households, is the basic unit for production as well as for dividing income and expenses; it controls its own human resources, animals, agricultural equipment, and section of land. For most day-to-day tasks a team is subdivided into work squads.

This organization pattern, however, merely describes the average. No rigid pattern has been set, so each commune as a whole is very flexible and can adapt to local circumstances.

According to Heiner Schweizer, who has made a comparison of the Chinese and Soviet agricultural systems, one important purpose of the Chinese people's communes is the systematic alleviation of the three basic ills of underdevelopment: unemployment, illiteracy, and lack of motivation.

By means of the communes China is putting work centers and simple industry in the country, so that the rural population can find employment without migrating to urban centers. Additionally, the communes improve the productivity of even that part of the rural population actually engaged in agriculture, since they can now keep busy during the slow season. In this way the average working time during the year has been extended from about 120 to almost 300 days, and the threat of overurbanization (with consequent crowding and unemployment or underemployment) is lessened.

This mobilization and organization of human resources has had a further important result: It has contributed to weaning the rural masses from their traditional lifestyle and patterns of thought, to liberating them from resignation, indifference, and passive acceptance of an authoritarian hierarchy. The people's communes were a radical blow to the gap between the modern modes of production and lifestyles in the industrial sector and the relatively backward organization of work and life on the land. Also largely eliminated were the arrogance and aloofness of Party and government officials, since these are now sent to the communes to be reeducated and become accustomed to manual labor.

Similarly, the commune system is destroying the traditional authoritarian family (already formally eliminated in 1950) and discrimination against women. The new attitude toward the family is often misunderstood in the West; in reality, the commune has not broken down the family but given it a new freedom. Provision is made for the different generations to live together. Women are pensioned at age 50, men at 60, but they continue to be part of the commune and, indeed, are highly respected members. Retired women chiefly take care of the households and of their grandchildren when the latter are not in school.

As for women, in old China they were strictly subject to their husbands' authority. Today, they are given full equality in the communes, sharing respect, authority, and the work load. (The last includes manual labor. In the fields and factories and dams, women work side by side with men.) They also have equal educational opportunities, and in China today they are represented in every profession. (In 1919 there was not a single female student in the Chinese universities; in 1972 almost one-quarter of the university professors and half the secondary-school students of China were women.) It must be admitted, however, that in the Chinese Communist Party and in the army, men still have the dominant role, although Mao has personally always fought for the emancipation of women.

In short, the communes are reorganizing Chinese society while immediately guaranteeing the necessities of life to the masses. Since 50 to 70 percent of each commune's agricultural yield is divided among its members, the rural population is sure of food as never before. Without the communes, China would have had catastrophically bad harvests during various recent droughts and floods; neither could its people have survived the sudden withdrawal of all economic aid by Soviet Russia in 1962.

Application to Other Developing Countries

Unemployment is already devastating in the developing countries and it appears that it will be their greatest problem in the years ahead. The people's communes have enabled China to eliminate unemployment while decentralizing. They have put an end to the great flight from the land that is still occurring in many developing countries. In China rural inhabitants can now continue to be an integral part of their communities and take part both in agricultural activity and in the increasingly extensive industrial productivity. Collectivization has also made it possible to get rid of hidden unemployment in the rural areas; people are no longer busy only during the planting and harvest seasons but have work to occupy them all year long. These new conditions have made it possible to eliminate various difficult social problems, such as alcoholism and prostitution.

Experience has shown that without the collectivization of agriculture the problems of unemployment, flight from the land, and swelling urbanization cannot be resolved.

15

THE NEW EDUCATION

In old China manual work was held in contempt, and there was a corresponding exaggerated respect for intellectuals. Proverbs and the sayings of respected wise men carried this prejudice from generation to generation. Mencius (372–289 B.C.), a famous successor of Confucius, was often quoted: "Use your mind, and you will rule; toil with your hands, and you will be ruled."

Mao realized that this tradition was a major hindrance to development and that elitism, as well as bureaucratism and dogmatism, had to be replaced by a new mentality. He therefore required that all Party members and army officers take an active part in productive work. "The officials of our Party and our State are ordinary workers, not masters riding the backs of the people. By taking part in the productive work done by the people as a whole, officials maintain close, comprehensive, and continuous contact with the workers" (Mao, 1964).

The creation of the people's communes in 1958 made this kind of solidarity possible and practical. With the Great Leap Forward officials were to share in the work of a commune and fulfill their obligations there; cadres, especially, were to pitch in. "If you're not a good worker, you're no official," said a popular slogan of the time, and at the beginning of the Great Leap a wave of enthusiasm for participation in manual work did indeed sweep across the country. Many cadres did a half day's work and a half day's manual toil; in addition, they took turns going as groups into the villages to help with the sowing, harvesting, and other agricultural tasks. These experiences led cadres to develop the "Five Abilities": 1) to see the problems work entails; 2) to know, through personal experience, what is possible and how it can be implemented; 3) to be able to hear what the peasants are saying; 4) to learn the wisdom, feelings, and skills of the working population; and 5) to be able to make the peasants see the importance of certain tasks from an ideological and political viewpoint.

Thus, between 1958 and 1965 various positive attitudes about life and education were instilled in a large proportion of Party members and bureaucrats: Manual work is an integral part of education and life; the proper reeducation of cadres can be accomplished through manual labor in the communes; the educational process, including most schools, should be transferred to the countryside.

But tradition was so strong that often bureaucratism and a false kind of authority began to creep back in. During the exciting upheaval of the revolution, Party members had lived among the people; now, after the victory, many had returned to their former position of dominance and lost their capacity for self-criticism. Even many students who had initially criticized the Party had fallen back gradually into elitism. And within the new younger generation, a large proportion of students were still coming from families of the former bourgeoisie or large landowners.

Mao and his followers believed this regression could destroy China's new development, and one purpose of the Great Proletarian Cultural Revolution was an attempt to bridge once again the seeming opposition between mental and physical work. Officials and students were once more sent into the countryside to learn "from the people and reality."

Soldiers, office workers, laborers, and peasants now must work directly with each other from time to time. They stand on the same ground, they work sharing the thoughts of Mao Tse-tung, and thus all, even with their apparent mutual contradictions, are bound together into a whole. The principle that binds them, that of producing through both mental and physical work, applies to each individual, even Mao himself. (According to reports, he grows his own vegetables.)

Education in China today must observe three basic principles: It must be highly practical; it must stimulate collective awareness and block individualism; it must be directed by the needs and goals of the people. From the very beginning of the school years young people have it drilled into them that school and learning are not ends in themselves and, indeed, are far less important than the socialist community spirit which enables people to overcome even the greatest obstacles.

Teachers, as Mao knows from experience, are persons in the service of the people. They have no reason to be proud of their knowledge, but do have the duty of making demands on their students. Authority, in the older understanding of the word, is now dead, and with it have gone conformism and learning by rote. For the future it is spontaneity, inventiveness, daring, experimentation, and the courage to take risks that will be rewarded. Everywhere in China there is the exhortation: "Have the courage to think, speak, and act! Down with unthinking authority!"

Today all Chinese children must attend school, but while in school they also continue to work in the factories. After the lower grades of primary school a three-year period of work determines who is to continue in education. Consequently, students for the university are chosen from the members of the communes, with the workers and peasants deciding who, in their judgment, deserves further studies. And a university student must regularly return to manual work on the land or in the factory.

In addition to furthering the melding of mental and manual labor, such a program prevents a surplus of academics. (From a sociological viewpoint, an "academic proletariat" tends to be conservative and thus does not promote further development.)

In 1972, 45 percent of the students were workers, with 40 percent coming from the agricultural sector and 15 percent from the army. All had at least three years of practical work behind them or an equal period of military service. One-fifth of all students were young women.

All education now has a practical orientation, even at the university level. For example, Hsui-Hua University has a series of factories and workshops. Old-style lectures have largely been replaced by study groups in which the subject matter is discussed and worked through by teachers and students together. Frequently engineers, master workers, and supervisors are brought in from industry to demonstrate the practical side of various subjects.

Additionally, studies in many areas have been boldly cut short and adapted to China's needs at its present stage of development. In medicine, for example, the much-publicized "barefoot doctors" are readied to start work after only about ten month's study. (For a more detailed examination of this program, see chapter 20.)

95

In speaking of China's new education, one must not forget its basic textbook—the thoughts of Mao Tse-tung. It is, of course, not only used in the formal schools but has become the people's reader. This was very important for the illiterate masses. Everyone wanted to be able to read it, and therefore everyone but a few old people have learned the basic 600 to 1,000 characters necessary to master it. In the course of a single generation a people of 700,000,000 became literate. The Mao primer thus brought about the greatest educational explosion in history, with age and social class playing no role in the process. Today almost everybody in China belongs to an organized study group.

The statements of Chairman Mao are like proverbs. They are not simply to be read or learned by rote; they are principles which enable the people to find new answers. Thus, study of this little book has not only taught the majority of the Chinese people to read; it has also led them to learn something they never knew before: how to apply criteria to specific situations. In this sense Mao's little book has produced a mass movement from a magical to an analytic mentality.

Application to Other Developing Countries

In the Chinese view, the greatest error Russia has made in its educational process has been to mistake the real situation, the real needs of the nation.

The same holds for the developing countries. Most of them have taken their school systems over wholesale from the West, and such systems have a built-in separation between an isolated upper class and the masses. But to serve development, education must serve the people, the country, and society.

The basic ill afflicting the developing countries' education shows up in the fact that the teacher is too distant from the student. In a Western-style school the students are isolated; they lose their roots in the people and become alienated from the realities of their own country. Elitist education is thus a barrier to development.

One way of eliminating such harmful tendencies is to connect mental and physical work systematically. In this process economic yield is not the primary consideration; rather the important thing is the educational effect.

Most developing countries today possess an unemployed intellectual proletariat which, in point of fact, is unemployed only because intellectuals are unwilling to work alongside the people. The traditional school of the West, which has been imported into the developing countries, gives chiefly a literary and philosophical education and neglects technical studies and the natural sciences. By linking education with work the Chinese have also linked the humanities with the natural sciences, as well as theory with practice. Education in China aims at forming a society and changing the individual's world so that everyone can live a truly human life.

Mao's little book illustrates a further point: The achievement of mass literacy requires textbooks that use the language of the people and speak to the concrete experience of the masses.

16

AGRICULTURE AS THE BASE

Perhaps Mao's greatest achievement is that he relied on the peasants and brought about the revolution with their help. He saw, early on, that true development would be impossible without their wholehearted participation. Yet during the pre-revolutionary period the agrarian question really threatened to split the Party, and in 1927 Mao was dismissed from the Party for his rural activity. Despite this, an All China Peasant Association was formed with Mao as its first chairman.

Throughout his active life Mao has again and again harked back to the importance of the poor peasants and their role in the revolution:

Stalin has said that "the national question is *virtually* a peasant question." That is to say, the Chinese revolution is virtually the peasants' revolution, and the resistance to Japan that is now going on is virtually the peasants' resistance to Japan. New democratic politics is virtually the granting of power to the peasants. . . . By "virtually" we mean essentially, not ignoring other factors. . . . It is common knowledge to every schoolboy that 80 percent of China's population are peasants. So the peasant problem has become the main problem of the Chinese revolution, and the strength of the peasants constitutes the principal force of the Chinese revolution. In the Chinese population the workers are second in size to the peasants [Mao, 1940].

Under Mao's leadership, therefore, the revolution of 1949 was a peasants' revolution. Unlike Lenin, who relied wholly on the workers (even though the peasants were a majority in Russia no less than in China), Mao wanted to and was able to make the peasants the basis of the revolution. By working with them, he was able, over time, to rouse them to political activity. He spoke of them with enthusiasm: "The peasants—the source of the Chinese army. . . . The peasants—the main force fighting for a democratic order in China at the present time" (Mao, 1945).

But despite Mao's belief in the peasants, he and his leadership did not find the right path immediately after the revolution. Some believed that a massive industrial effort had to be made immediately; others wanted to effect a land reform first and "then to serve agriculture." Only in 1958's Great Leap Forward was the proper emphasis found: "Agriculture is the basis, industry the leading factor in the economy." In other words, the rhythm of industrial development had to be adapted to the rhythm of agriculture, and industrial production had to meet the needs of agriculture. Simultaneously, the creation of the communes linked agriculture and industry more closely.

It is characteristic of the Chinese development model that even when emphasis was placed on agriculture, little capital was invested in it; rather, enormous amounts of human effort were used to accomplish near miracles. Great irrigation and drainage projects were undertaken. By 1955 the pre-war availability of water in the countryside had been restored: of 259,350,000 acres of arable land about one-quarter was being artificially irrigated. Simultaneously, great afforestation projects were begun. Since one purpose of these is to prevent erosion, they were first undertaken on the hills that bordered the farmland. Penetration into mountainous or desert wastes had to wait till a later time.

Mao was repeatedly able to stir the gradually wearying peasants to new efforts. In 1964 he issued the great summons: "Learn from Tachai!" (The unassuming northern village, described in chapter 1, whose early communal spirit, enormous feats in combatting meagre natural resources, and balanced development have made it the example and model for the entire country). In answer, the peasants everywhere competed with one another in the revolutionary spirit of that model village. The results were phenomenal.

Take, for example, the work of Hoengsheng (in the province of Hopei, 279 miles south of Peking). In five winters of hard work, starting in 1965, the peasants leveled over 80 hills, filled up more than 200 depressions or holes, and converted about 395 acres of arable land into garden-like fields. At the same time they improved the very sandy and salty ground. In 1959 the community had only one electrically powered well; today it has forty-one. The peasants' dense network of canals and ditches makes the irrigation and drainage system highly effective.

Accomplishments such as these all over the country have given agricultural development a strong material basis. The grain reserves of the State, the communes, the production brigades and teams, as well as of individual families, are eloquent testimony to the increasing capability of Chinese agriculture. In 1971 (a year of bad drought) China harvested 246,000,000 tons of grain; in 1967 it had been 230,000,000 tons. Figuring the population at 750,000,000 (which may be a high estimate) such harvests give each inhabitant over 660 pounds of grain a year—a good deal more than is required for sustenance. Anyone who knew the old China will tell you that the sight of a full grain bin in the home of a Chinese peasant almost challenges belief. There is still much to do, of course, but "on the whole," says the British Sinologist Derek Bryan, "Chinese agriculture is probably more effective than that of Western Europe." It is, in addition, ecologically more sound, since it uses mostly human and animal excrement as fertilizer.

Fertilization is actually an excellent example of the relationship between the needs of agriculture and the growth of industrial production under the Chinese model of development.

In the early days of the revolution, an enormous amount of work went into fertilizing. As long as the shoulder-pole was the only means of transportation, preparation and application of compost material required 30 to 40 percent of the total labor devoted to agriculture. Today mechanization has come a long way in China, and much of it is used for agricultural purposes. Most of the approximately 74,000 communes have small factories for producing artificial fertilizers, as well as agricultural equipment and machinery. The efforts to improve the soil continue. Thus, in 1972 irrigated acreage was extended by 8,151,000 acres.

Application to Other Developing Countries

Many developing countries have made efforts to develop agriculture solely through mechanization, without any attention to consciousness-raising. Additionally, there has been industrialization and modernization, but insufficient concern with agriculture.

In most developing countries land reform is a necessary prerequisite of healthy development. Large plantations and an unjust system of tenancy mean that neither landlord nor peasant is interested in increasing productivity: the former, because he already has too much; the latter, because he will not be better off for it.

Peasants may tend to be conservative, yet the Chinese revolution has shown that they are quite capable of revolution if their own interests are honestly taken into account by it.

17

LOCAL INDUSTRY AND TECHNOLOGICAL ADAPTATION

As we have seen, agriculture still provides the broad base of the Chinese economy. Simultaneously both heavy and light industry is being developed, but its aim is, in large measure, to provide machinery and tools for the agricultural sector. Industrial development is being used to establish agricultural-industrial communities that are largely self-sufficient; it is also designed to educate the peasant masses in a new worldview. Under the principle of self-help, the state subsidizes neither agriculture nor local industry; they themselves must find the means of producing needed equipment and processing raw materials.

China is divided into about 2000 regions, half of which at any given time possess all five basic industries: machinery plants, chemical plants, cement works, coal mines and iron and steel works.

Today, steel is manufactured not only in the large state-controlled and state-financed steel works, but also in small factories in the communes and provincial towns. The output of these factories is intended exclusively to meet local needs, especially the manufacture and repair of simple farm machinery.

Local industry also produces artificial fertilizer, cement, and simple means of transportation, and processes farm products. Small-scale generating plants are also to be found almost everywhere in China.

This kind of local industry is intended as a complement to agriculture, an approach to development that Mao described in 1958 as "walking on both legs." As we have seen, this phrase indicates a linking of contraries and refers to the concurrent use of traditional and modern technologies and the simultaneous development of industry and agriculture, national and local industries, heavy and light industries, and small, medium, and large enterprises. (See chapters 7 and 10 for further discussion of the philosophical bases for this policy.)

"Walking on both legs" with an emphasis on local development often means that the technical level of much industry is not very high. It is, however, highly functional and adapted to local conditions. In other words, the quality is high enough to meet the need.

There are several reasons for this acceptance of

rather simple technology and less-than-top quality. First, as we have seen, it has made it possible to promote decentralized industrialization of a large country with an enormous peasant population while maintaining agriculture as the economic and developmental base. Second, it is a practical approach for a country where even the transportation and communications networks are relatively backward. It avoids the problems of very up-to-date machinery, which depends on outside sources for replacement parts and could lead to lengthy delays and serious production lags in the event of breakdowns. Third, it serves an educational function for the masses.

This approach is so non-Western that it is often misunderstood in the West. Take, for example, the "Iron Competition" of 1958, an early example of local industrialization that became known in the West and was met with pitying laughter. During four months, starting in July 1958, about a million small smelting furnaces were built in the villages. Since every province of China has at least small deposits of iron ore and somewhat larger deposits of coal, groups all over the country could—and did—take part in the effort. By late autumn travelers reported that at night light from the smelting fires could be seen all over China. What bemused Westerners was the fact that these furnaces were all of a preindustrial type, and that "Operation Village Iron" disappeared after six months to a year. During their short lives the furnaces had produced an average of only ten tons of iron apiece, and about half of that had been usable only for manufacturing that required very low-quality iron.

Western critics calculated that this romantic enterprise cost China a billion dollars. But the Chinese leaders looked at the whole operation differently. They had been concerned with goals other than profit or industrialization per se. The villages where the operation had been mounted were populated by peasants whose thinking over the centuries had been primarily magical. These sorry smelting furnaces had been a first contact with industrial technology and had taught them to think in terms of cause and effect. People whose whole outlook had been formed by tradition had become acquainted with a simple technology for industrial production. They had undergone an experience that radically changed their worldview. And, in addition to these educational gains, the experiment had also uncovered numerous rural inhabitants who had technical gifts which had never had a chance to be brought to light. With the help of the individuals thus discovered and with the use of the good iron supplied by the villages, several thousand industrial-type blast furnaces were built as early as 1959 in numerous localities; the large state-owned foundries also lent a helping hand in the project. In 1960 several hundred medium-size blast furnaces were built in the same way. Thus the Chinese leaders were able to develop the iron and steel industry all over the country and to involve a large part of the population in the doing of it.

The development of local iron and steel works is not only a good example of how China has decentralized its industry; it also demonstrates how industrialization has been used as a learning process. Using a moderately advanced technology that is adapted to the workers' capacities and that takes account of local conditions, China has proceeded step by step, constantly on guard lest technology outstrip the human beings involved or society as a whole. In China technology is not regarded as something predetermined, a machine or escalator to which the individual and society must adapt and yield. Rather, it is seen as something to be adapted to the human needs of society.

Thus, "walking on both legs" means a step-by-step transition from the old technology (which was, in part, very unproductive) to new methods that truly aid the people, especially the peasants. For example, carrying-poles are rapidly being replaced by simple handcarts as a key means of transport. Now the pushcart does not represent a very high level of technology, but it is effecting a real revolution in Chinese agriculture and, therefore, the Chinese life. The most that one person can transport with a carrying-pole in one day is 990 pounds over 1 kilometer; with a pushcart the figure rises to 1,760 pounds, and, if the cart has pneumatic tires, the latter amount doubles.

Similarly local industry is also making it possible to install simple waterpumps wherever needed. These cheap, almost primitive machines are playing an important role in extending effective irrigation.

Further examples of technology that is adapted to economic conditions and real needs are small water-powered plants, implements for rice cultivation, treadle-powered threshing machines, and hand-powered husking machines. In constructing many of these aids, locally obtained raw materials, such as wood and bamboo, can be used.

Although China's path toward industrialization is laying much stress on development of such local industry in the rural areas, the urban sector is not being neglected. Indeed, since the Cultural Revolution district factories in the cities have grown very quickly. In Nanking, for example, there are reported to be over 500 such factories and production associations today, employing 20,000 workers and other staff—75 percent of them women. (The role of women in Chinese industry today is so great that a phenomenon has sprung up of housewives founding and running factories. The *Peking Review* [March 12, 1973] reports that in Nanking a number of such establishments are making progress.) These urban district factories usually begin as improvised ventures and are gradually improved into full-fledged plants. Today they produce more than a thousand different products and are an important supplement to state-managed industry. The emphasis, as in agricultural-industrial communes, is on light industry turning out products of real use to the people: synthetic fabric and cleansers, sewing machines, bicycles, wristwatches and the like.

The path of industrialization in China is thus turning out to be a process of liberation—very unlike the nineteenth-century development in the West, where industrialization often meant the enslavement rather than the emancipation of people. Decentralized industrialization is a popular movement and the Chinese press is constantly reporting experiments and successes in it. Those involved in it are learning from every experience. Everyone is urged to study, criticize, think, and act.

Application to Other Developing Countries

China's experiences can be very important for most other developing countries, for it has successfully discovered ways of keeping the rural population busy and productive in both the agricultural and industrial sectors. In building its economy step by step, it has been able to accumulate and evaluate numerous experiences and has not needed to take over outside technology sight unseen. There are risks involved, but such experimental techniques have been relatively easy to adopt in a closed society with collectivized agriculture and industry. The existence of associations also favors the spread of new technologies.

The introduction of medium-complexity technology also has had an educational effect. Mao puts it aptly: "There can be two attitudes to learning. One is dogmatic and consists in taking over everything, whether or not it is really suitable in the conditions of our country. That is an unprofitable attitude. The other consists in applying the mind to study and mastering everything that fits in with conditions in our country, in other words, evaluating all experiences that are useful for us."

In this sense, medium-complexity technology and decentralized industrialization tied to real needs are key factors for a genuine development.

18

DEURBANIZATION

Most developing countries today helplessly watch thousands or millions of their peasants moving to the cities, where most often they find no work and end up swelling the impoverished, marginal ghettoes. In China this is no longer happening. Thanks to the development of decentralized industrialization with a technology that answers immediate human needs, the Chinese peasants can find sufficient work in the rural areas.

In fact, in China today the population movement is from city to country, so that the number of city dwellers has decreased to some extent. An estimated twelve million people have already moved from the overcrowded cities and settled in rural areas, especially in the broad, empty regions of western China. According to China expert Edgar Snow, a million people have emigrated from Shanghai alone since 1965.

Jean-Paul Rüttimann, the Swiss development

expert, has pointed out that for most countries the problems of urbanization and unemployment will, in the long run, prove more difficult than the problem of hunger. In China, realization of this fact had produced corrective actions by 1958 if not sooner. In announcing the policies of the Great Leap Forward, Mao said: "By 'urbanization of the countryside and ruralization of the cities' we seek to express the fact that society as a whole is undergoing a new transformation."

By the time of the Cultural Revolution the opposition of city and countryside had become a pressing problem once again. It was necessary that the cities, which were threatening to become gathering places of "revisionists and parasites," should once more learn a lesson from the rural areas. So, as Chou En-lai said:

The most capable of the big city cadres will go to various locations in the province, or have already gone there, in order to strengthen the right type of leadership. There, many will be required to help in the management of industries and institutes that at an earlier time were directly under the central government but now have been put under the local administration. Many of the members are over sixty and ready to be pensioned off. Some of them will live with their families in communes. There will be enough work for all.

Thus, deurbanization policy was traceable to intensified efforts toward regional and local independence, both in the provision of food and in industrialization. And, for practical and educational reasons, the urban exodus was not restricted to the masses; there were also organized transfers of educated young people and adults from the large cities to both regional centers and people's communes in the interior.

Mao and his leadership have a deep philosophical reason for emphasizing deurbanization: They cultivate the utopian dream of being able some day to eliminate cities completely. The reason is that for them the cities are the symbol and fortress of the once dominant class; they are the offspring of capitalism and imperialism, which have left their mark in the form of banks, insurance agencies, office buildings, and trading houses. With the fall of the rulers, the city, too, must disappear. At present, city-dwellers and rural population are distinguished by a simple test: Those who buy grain are urban, those who produce it are rural. In the Maoists' view, the people who work in the cities are, whether they want to be or not, alienated, revisionist, bureaucratic, and elitist. They have been separated from the totality and are therefore a kind of "waste"; integration is possible only via the land and the communes.

Application to Other Developing Countries

In many developing countries the migration to the cities has become a flood, and the resultant unemployment, transformation of residential areas into slums, and pauperization of the newcomers have all become uncontrollable. For example, it is estimated that in the year 2000, Calcutta—already a teeming boil of unemployment, crowding, and misery with 5 million inhabitants—will have between 36 and 66 million inhabitants if the present rate of growth is not checked.

If we reflect further on the enormous social cost of the urban conglomerates in the United States, Europe, the Soviet Union, and Japan, then the few developing countries that are carefully studying China's urban and industrial policies are following the right track. Many economists believe that the kind of industrialization which depends on huge urban centers is a largely irreversible process. In the Chinese model, on the other hand, urbanization is controlled, decentralization takes the pressure off the transportation system, seasonal unemployment disappears, and local industrialization is made possible.

19

NO WASTE
IN CHINA

China's utopian dream of a country without cities has not yet been realized, and may well never be. China still has numerous urban areas, some of them very large, but they are cities with a difference, cities at peace with the human and natural environment.

In the other great urban centers of the East—Bombay, Calcutta, Hong Kong, Tokyo —population and traffic, poverty and chaos, refuse and exhaust fumes increase daily in almost geometric progression. The cities of China, on the contrary, no longer have ghettoes of poverty and filth. They are full of trees and open green spaces; there are almost no automobiles or pollution; they are very busy places but also very orderly.

Shortly after the revolution, China started to dismantle the old cities, which had become the refuse-pits of capitalism, and to build them new from the ground up. Beginning in 1958, the Great Leap Forward, with its emphasis on deurbanization and the rational building of a new society, gave the construction of decent urban centers a further boost. For example, the population of Shanghai, the largest city, increased from 4.1 to 7.5 million from 1949 to 1958, but between 1958 and 1965, it increased by only 0.7 million more. The development of the people's communes and local industry had stopped too-rapid growth.

In other words, China solved the problem of urbanization, with its accompanying environmental difficulties, not by superficial treatment but by a radical cure, by methods that really went to the root of the problem.

China's Approach to the Problem of the Environment

For this reason and others, China's claims to know some answers at the United Nations Conference on the Environment (Stockholm, June 1972) were not "just communist propaganda." In its "Declaration on a Human Environment" China pointed quite clearly to the social causes of environmental pollution, to the connections among the arms race, war, population growth, and the preservation or protection of the environment. It pointed especially to the Third World's need to guard national resources and to its struggle against being overwhelmed by foreign cultures and tourists. The speech of the Chinese delegate did not please many Westerners or governments in developing countries (for rather different reasons), but what he said did hit the mark:

The basic problem in the effort to protect the environment is the capitalist system of consumption. . . . Imperialist wars of aggression have done the greatest harm to the environment. Imperialism, colonialism, and neo-colonialism have. . . destroyed human culture and civilization and laid waste to the environment in which human life must be lived. . . . Some highly developed countries have not only seriously polluted their own environment but have also destroyed the environment in other countries and done it general harm on a global scale.

In the Chinese view Russia betrayed the revolution at the moment when it began to imitate the West, when it no longer knew how to unite opposites, when it entered upon a lopsided development that was disruptive and finally destructive of the environment.

China has traveled a different road. It has sought to get at the root of things, to look at all sides, to see things positively and negatively, to acknowledge and accept both good and evil, to preserve in the midst of tension or—to put it in Chinese terms—to live dialectically. Thus, modern China is attempting to deal with its reality in a global way and not to fragment it, isolate the parts, and break them up into smaller and smaller pieces. For the Chinese believe that just as fertile land becomes barren if continually divided and subdivided, so society suffers if it is broken up into isolated individuals.

China is building upon this intellectual or philosophical approach to reality. Its methods of industrialization, urbanization, and environmental protection must be understood against this conceptual background.

As a practical application of China's dialectic approach, factories were moved from the coastal cities to villages in the interior. At the same time, the effort was made to build waste reprocessing industries around the areas where production gave rise to harmful waste products. In this way, industry was relocated among the people. In this way also, the dangerous poisoning of city and countryside was significantly lessened. One example among countless others:

Workers and technicians at the chemical fertilizer factory in Nanking have made significant progress in finding numerous uses for waste water, exhaust gas, and other residues. In the past three years 46,000 tons of usable materials have been recovered. Six million yuan worth of nickel, raw iron, aluminum sulfate, and sodium silicate were retrieved from wastes. Exhaust gases yielded sulphuric acid; hydrogen was separated from these same gases, and in an experiment they were made to yield hydroxalic sulfate. In addition waste heat was used to generate 4,000,000 kilowatt hours of electricity [*Peking Review*, July 11, 1972].

The efforts to reduce industrial pollution are

probably made easier by the fact that the Chinese, throughout their history, have always attempted never to waste anything. The traditional view is that even the negative can be used in a positive way: That is precisely humanity's special art.

But the modern application of this principle is very much part of modern China's road to a new society. Chinese industrialization began with the person in mind. The community is in the foreground of consciousness. This means that all the people, not just a thin upper stratum, count. The drive for industrialization is not derived from a Westernized elite that imports automobiles, color television sets, and automatic washing machines, as happens in other developing countries. Even today there are hardly any luxuries for anyone in China. Everyone is poor, but everyone is equal; differences between people are slight; poverty is shared by everyone and is thus bearable. Everyone and everything is integrated into the whole. Consequently, there is no waste: no waste produced by prosperity and no "wasted" human beings.

Application to Other Developing Countries

Most of the developing countries believe, even today, that they have no environmental problems. They regard concern for the environment as a concern necessary only to the rich nations of East and West. Their own first concern is for survival. Yet by impulsive imitation of Western methods they may be letting themselves in, unsuspectingly, for the waste that characterizes these methods: For this reason alone they ought to be aware of the environmental problem right from the beginning. In many of these countries it may already be too late to follow the Chinese model; in the others it is high time to choose paths that will lead to the least possible waste of materials and people.

20

PEASANT AND DOCTOR

In 1965 Chairman Mao criticized the Ministry of Health as an "urban overlord" and demanded that medicine shift its main focus to the villages. His statement led to revolutionary changes in the delivery of health care and the education of medical personnel. For example, in the special administrative region of Peking, which has a population of about 6 million and includes ten surburban districts with 280 people's communes, there are now seventeen commune hospitals ånd thirty district hospitals, totaling 29,000 beds. The region has at its disposal over 8,600 students at a medical school, and about 2,000 doctors practicing traditional medicine. As a result of Mao's challenge, 3,600 doctors and workers for the Health Authority have gone out from Peking into the countryside during the last few years.

A particularly striking response to the 1965 call for the Cultural Revolution was the development of new methods of delivering health care, especially to the countryside. One was the creation of "mobile medical teams," in which doctors, nurses, and cadres are assigned to take turns at working in rural areas. A representative of the Health Authority describes the task of these teams:

to serve the people directly by applying preventative or therapeutic measures and thus laying stress on health maintenance; to train basic medical personnel in the various localities; to spread the idea of family planning; to raise the present level of health care; to combine traditional and Western methods; to promote revolutionary socialist thinking among medical workers so that they will live with workers, peasants, and soldiers, eat the same food, work in the same manner, study along with them, and learn to criticize the bourgeois way of life.

In Peking alone about 6,000 doctors and other health workers (about one-third of its total medical personnel) work in these rotating groups. Organized into 430 teams, they have gone as far as Szechuan, Yunnan, and Inner Mongolia.

An even more radical approach to the problem of delivering health care has been the creation of a new kind of health worker, educated under a new system and tackling the work in a new way that is particularly typical of the revolutionary social system. These are the "barefoot doctors," so called because they work barefoot alongside the peasants in the rice fields. Chosen from among the peasant population, they work among the peasants in a people's commune. At intervals they may leave the countryside to increase their medical knowledge, but most of the time—and especially during the seeding and harvest periods—they are in the village, exercising three functions: peasant, doctor, and health specialist for the people.

The education of the "barefoot doctor" is a complete departure from the traditional system. After being selected from a commune, the students attend a training period which lasts from three to ten months; part of this will be in a city, but, whenever possible, part will be in the commune's own local hospital. After the initial training period, the "barefoot doctors" have a basic knowledge of anatomy and Western and Chinese medicine; they know how to diagnose and treat about seventy-five common diseases, to prescribe perhaps one hundred kinds of medicine, and to apply the basic rules of acupuncture to thirty important areas of the human body. Armed with this training, a chest of medicines, and *The Thoughts of Chairman Mao*, the neophytes are now ready to go out among the people. They will return for further training during the next three years, but meanwhile they work at both agriculture and health care.

The training of these "barefoot doctors" follows the principle of combining theory and practice and of providing sufficient knowledge for a job as efficiently as possible. The aim is to develop, as quickly as possible, the ability to do practical work and to lay a foundation for further training in the future. The training is done in groups and centers around the concrete, everyday problems of a doctor.

The first "barefoot doctors" appeared shortly after the beginning of the Cultural Revolution, when about 30,000 working teams of doctors were sent into villages all over China to train selected peasants. The government reports that there are now about a million of these specially trained health specialists, working with the peasants throughout China's extensive rural areas. The special region of Peking alone boasts 13,000. They include both men and women; their average age is twenty.

In addition to the "barefoot doctors," China has another new kind of health worker. These are the "red-worker-doctors," who function somewhat like ambulance personnel. They are assigned to city or factory clinics or to the People's Liberation Army.

With these sorts of innovations China, which had suffered from very underdeveloped public health services in the past, is now able to deliver health care in nearly sufficient quantity. Since the People's Republic was established, twenty-six times more persons have received medical and other health-service training than in the twenty years before liberation. Medical science and technology are developing constantly, and today China is basically self-sufficient in medicines, medical instruments, and biological products.

Even more important than the quantity of health care available is the fact that the innovative use of personnel, such as the barefoot doctors, means that it can be delivered when and where needed even throughout the vast countryside. Simple cases can be treated in the patient's village home or at the brigade clinic, more serious ones in the commune hospital. Only the most complicated cases are turned over to city hospitals.

The improvements in public health are closely linked to the development of the revolutionary social spirit among the masses. Not only is full use made of medical resources, not only are health-care personnel encouraged in various ways to work side by side with the people. In addition the masses themselves have been mobilized for the struggle against sickness and unhygienic conditions. There are patriotic hygiene groups throughout the country; their aim is to eliminate the four main causes of disease: flies, gnats, mice, and bugs. With their help scourges such as smallpox, plague, cholera, kala-azar (a common tropical infection), and venereal diseases have now been eradicated. Various infectious diseases, illness caused by parasites, and other endemic illnesses have been lessened significantly.

In the Chinese tradition health is connected with functional bodily harmony of the two basic contrary energies, Yang and Yin. Sickness is the result of a disordered relationship between various organs and the areas that surround them. Healing consists in restoring the lost balance by relieving tension among the four opposites: negative/positive, outward/inward, hot/cold, and empty/full. Mao's disciples have taken this tradition and applied it to the social body as well as the physical body.

The great exemplar of the revolution and medicine is the Canadian doctor, Norman Bethune, who is regarded as a hero in China because he took part personally in the Chinese revolution and devoted himself to building a new society. "Comrade Bethune's spirit of doing everything for others' benefit and nothing for his own was shown in his extreme sense of responsibility in his work and his extreme warmheartedness towards his comrades and the people" (Mao).

China is, of course, still a developing country, but shifting the focus of medical care to the villages and tying public health care with mass movements have resulted in the masses of peasants and workers receiving proper medical care.

Application to Other Developing Countries

China's experience shows that developing countries can develop their health services rather quickly, even if the base is relatively weak at the beginning.

The "barefoot doctor" idea could be taken over in many countries. It presupposes only a short, practical training. This quick and effective method counters the disadvantages of traditional medical schools. The latter are not only unable to turn out a large number of doctors in a short time; they also contribute to alienating students from their habitual environment, making them unwilling to return to the rural areas after their training.

An old Chinese saying suggests what the developing countries must do to overcome the lag in medical care and hygiene in rural areas: "In snowy weather to throw more coal on the fire, not to add another flower to the tapestry." "Barefoot doctors" and other practical innovations are a new force with a great future.

21

POPULATION
CONTROL

The problem of population control exists in China, as in all developing countries, but China has made great progress in this area. Nonetheless, it must be prepared to feed and employ about a billion people in the year 2000.

Already China is the most populous country in the world. It has three times the population of the Soviet Union, four times that of the United States. Until a short time ago, China also had a very high birth rate: 25 per every 1000 inhabitants, while the death rate was 12 per 1000. As a result China had each year about 15,000,000 more births than deaths.

In 1973, Ti Lung, substitute delegate to the United Nations Economic Conference for Asia and the Far East, spoke on the population problem and China's policy:

Planned population growth is a firm policy in China. We apply such a policy, not because China has a problem of overpopulation, but because social production is developing in a planned way and this requires a planned population growth. Planned population growth is also necessary if women are to be fully liberated, women, mothers, and children to be protected, the upcoming generation properly educated, the health of the people improved, and national prosperity to be achieved. This policy is in tune with the interests and wishes of the broad masses [U.N. Economic Conference for Asia and the Far East, 29th session, April 16, 1973].

Ti Lung insisted that China had no overpopulation problem. A population of 700 million averages to 760 persons per square mile, about the average for Europe. But even after intensive deurbanization the distribution is still very unequal; two-thirds of the Chinese live in one-sixth of the total area. Consequently there is still plenty of room for growth; the problem is one of distribution and decentralization.

The population problem must also be seen in the context of available food (in China, chiefly grain production). According to Ti Lung, the average annual growth rate in China's population since the establishment of the People's Republic has been about 2 percent, while the growth rate in grain production has been almost 4 percent. Moreover, the area presently cultivated (about 247,000,000 acres) amounts to only a little more than one-tenth of the total land surface.

Nevertheless, as Ti Lung's statement makes clear, the Chinese leadership believes population control is a necessary part of developing the new social order. Family planning began in 1962 with the recommendation of late marriage and two children per family. The recommendations met some, but by no means total, success. Age-old Chinese tradition was—and still is—an obstacle to family planning. So today there is a massive effort to bring the implications of having too many children home to the people. Simple and clear explanations show the significance of the child in terms of the economy, culture, education, living standard, health, and employment. Slogans are used to make ideas stick: "Only exploiters think of children as private property!" "Uncontrolled births are due to habits inherited or taken over from the old society!" "We may no longer look on children as provision for our old age, as people hoard grain against famine. Today *we plan!*"

Administration and social organizations at all levels are using such propaganda and more explicit education to mobilize the masses for a deliberate application of family planning. The state provides the means of birth control free, as well as appropriate medical assistance. The pill is distributed to women free, right in the factories. The campaign for late marriages (women no earlier than age 26, men age 28) continues and is closely connected with the birth control effort.

The Chinese leaders have always put the population problem—like most others—into economic, social, and political terms. Now and then, observers get the feeling that the revolution's intensive propaganda and consciousness-raising processes are leading the people to win and till new land and to increase the communes' industrial production rather than to practice family planning. But it must be admitted that even in this fashion the Chinese have certainly sublimated a great deal of sexual energy.

Alberto Moravia, the Italian author of *The Red Book and the Great Wall: An Impression of Mao's China*, is struck by the way continence and chastity are preached as a form of health maintenance. "Poverty and chastity, if you think about it, are the two normal conditions of man, or at least they ought to be in the world today." According to Moravia, love in China leads not to sexual relations but to chastity. The reason is that, through the communes, China has placed the individual within a larger framework, with the result that life has acquired a new meaning for him or her. The important thing now is not simply children and their survival, but the new society that will live on through justice.

Application to Other Developing Countries

The high birth rate in many developing countries eats up whatever economic growth is achieved. But a propaganda campaign in favor of birth control will have little effect if medicine is isolated from the overall social context. China is proof that the problem must be put in a larger context and turned chiefly into a mass movement, rather than a campaign directed at individuals.

Developed countries can also learn a psychological lesson from China in this area. Very often the approach to the population problem is much too negative and produces results opposite to the intended effect. Overpopulation cannot be eliminated if it is regarded as an isolated issue. Simultaneously the liberation of women must be emphasized and individuals' lives directed more to public concerns. In this way population control becomes more than a private effort on the part of individuals; it serves society, and this must be realized.

22

POVERTY—
EQUALLY
DISTRIBUTED

When the Italian author Alberto Moravia visited China during the Cultural Revolution, he was fascinated by a society that showed neither pauperization nor prosperity but was controlled by the ideal of complete equality. In China he met a new dimension of poverty. It is a poverty that cannot be contrasted with wealth because it is self-contained and has to do with the quality of life rather than possession of consumer goods. The complete absence of wealth and the egalitarian poverty of a whole people seemed proof to Moravia that a utopia of complete equality has been created. China has been able to give a new meaning to poverty, since it has shown that the necessary conditions for becoming a true human being are present even in poverty: nothing more and nothing less.

China has, of course, made great strides toward material wealth, but by Western standards it is still poor. The poverty is bearable, however, because it is the normal condition. For Moravia, the Chinese experience could be summed up by saying that in the People's Republic brotherhood and equality are truly more important than prosperity.

According to H. Dickinson, a representative of the World Council of Churches, there is no doubt that prosperity is increasing in China and that what material wealth exists is equally distributed as in no other country of the world. Heiner Schweizer also comes to the conclusion that in China income is probably much more equally distributed than in any other country. The pie to be shared is still a small one, but at least all share it equally.

The practice of equality certainly makes poverty more bearable; it also liberates energy for pushing the frontiers of general poverty back even further. Certainly leaders who share poverty can require greater efforts from the people than can leaders who live in luxury while the masses are poor.

The Chinese look on the people's communes as a specific way to level the differences between rich and poor, as well as between workers and peasants. As the basis for local industrialization, the commune brings all kinds of people together and makes them mingle, sharing goods, ideas, and goals.

The whole aim of socialism or communism can be summed up as creating a state of equality between peasants, workers, and intellectuals. In China after the revolution, the peasants were in the worst situation; therefore, the first effort had to be to help them. That goal was approached in a series of steps.

1. The land tax, which was 12 percent at the beginning of the 1950s, was reduced to 7 percent (and in some cases, such as communes which depend heavily on easily perishable produce, to 4 percent). This has enabled the communes to build up capital and to repay modest loans.

2. The state purchase price for certain agricultural products, such as sugar cane, sugar beets, oil products, and bast fiber, was increased, with specification that the additional gain was to go directly to the commune members. This both stimulated agricultural production and increased the peasants' income.

3. The cost of electricity was set 40 percent cheaper for agriculture than for industry, with the state making up the difference. This stimulates modernization and increased production in the agricultural communes.

4. Communes which lack capital are encouraged to build machinery themselves. This encourages self-help, as well as local industrialization and increased production.

5. The price of certain consumer goods—for example, medicines and leather shoes—was lowered.

As a result of these and many other measures, the living standard of the masses, which means chiefly the peasants, is rising gradually. After eight years of agricultural advance, most people now believe in the reality of the promised "Five Guarantees": food, shelter and clothing, fuel, medical care, and proper burial. "Adequate?" Edgar Snow writes in *The Long Revolution*. "China's communes are very poor. . . . The livelihood they provide is 'adequate,' however, far beyond the former dreams of the landless and perennially overworked, hungry illiterates who were most of the peasants in pre-revolutionary China."

The paradoxical fact that, despite increased industrial and agricultural capability and despite the availability of all important consumer goods, the material aspect of life is becoming increasingly less important in China makes clear what a vision has been able to accomplish and how a world outlook can turn values around. Families have sufficient food, clothing, and houses or other types of dwellings. Living conditions do still leave much to be desired, especially in the cities. But Derek Bryan, secretary of the British Legation, can write: "The Chinese people are in no danger of becoming a consumer society. . . . We can predict with assurance that the investment needed to raise the Chinese living standard will become increasingly smaller, and China's surplus will be given in ever greater measure to other countries as assistance for development."

One method of ensuring the Chinese vision of equality is that differences in salary are very small. The pilot of a commercial jet liner earned about $30.00 a month in 1972, but his stewards or stewardesses made only about $5.40 less. Foreign visitors are also struck by the fact that members of the Party committees frequently earn less than skilled workers.

The Cultural Revolution was chiefly concerned with equality. It was a revolt against new elites, a new wealthy class, a new group of bureaucrats, and people who thought in terms of growth. A new social order is being built in which there is no room for the wealthy. The oppositions between city and countryside, men and women, physical and intellectual work, and, above all, between rich and poor, are being eliminated. As Peter W. Frey, a Swiss journalist, puts it, the Chinese are poor, "but no longer paupers, and the step from pauperism to poverty is a decisive one in terms of human dignity" (*Tages-Anzeiger Magazin*, no. 46, 1972).

Application to Other Developing Countries

The question of income distribution is becoming ever more prominent. The debate has not stopped since Robert McNamara referred to this sore point at UNCTAD III. It is especially evident that development aid has often only widened the distance between rich and poor. "To him who has, more will be given" evidently holds in this area, too.

China has approached the problem of internal equity in a way quite different from that of most developing—and developed—countries. It did not first simply make the pie bigger, with a view to somehow distributing it later on. Instead, it went right to the root of the matter and started with equalizing the distribution of what it had. The Cultural Revolution was a reaction to a threatening loss of ideals. And the words of Chairman Mao and the other leaders about egalitarianism can be taken seriously because they themselves live very modestly.

The Chinese experience also shows that it may be impossible to eradicate poverty. But perhaps far more important than such an eradication is the willingness to share the poverty that exists. Poverty becomes unbearable chiefly when it stands in sharp contrast to wealth and extravagance.

23

SOLIDARITY WITH THE POOR OF THE WORLD

In the eyes of the Chinese the most important conflict is not between imperialism and socialism but between imperialism and the oppressed Third World. This conviction gives rise to a different strategy from that pursued by the Soviet Union. The Soviet Union is all for peaceful coexistence and competition, but China thinks of itself as participant in a guerrilla war for the liberation of all peoples.

As the Chinese see it, no developing country can solve the problems of underdevelopment without help. The essential causes of underdevelopment are exploitation, neocolonialism, and the imperialist exercise of power. But if the underdeveloped peoples help each other, they can throw off their false dependencies.

The Chinese delegates to international organizations never tire of repeating, "It was the blood and sweat of the Third World peoples that made possible the beginnings of modern capitalism." "Imperialist and colonial suppression inflicted terrible distress on the Africans and plunged the continent into darkness for a long time. But where there is suppression, there can also be resistance."

China is constantly proclaiming that it shares the struggle of the Third World countries against imperialism, colonialism, and neocolonialism, and that it wants solidarity with these countries once they reach freedom.

Chairman Mao writes: "There are difficulties and problems everywhere, and we [Chinese] must help overcome or solve them. We will go to share the work and the struggle."

Because of this belief, the People's Republic, though itself a developing country, has been giving help to others for years. Africa and Asia have received the most attention, with priority going to the building of roads, railroads, power plants, model farms, irrigation systems, and textile factories. The Chinese insist that all projects must be adapted to local circumstances.

In 1964 Premier Chou En-lai laid down eight principles for aid; they were derived from the experience of development in China itself. These principles are 1) aid ought to profit both parties; 2) no political or economic conditions should be set down for granting or receiving such help; 3) normally loans should be interest free; 4) aid should promote true economic development, aiming at making the recipient independent of the donor as quickly as possible; 5) normally aid projects should have small investment requirements but be labor intensive; 6) generosity should be shown if a recipient has difficulty in repaying; 7) supplies should be purchased from China at world market prices; and 8) the Chinese experts who participate in a foreign aid project should accept the standard of living usual for the native population of the host country.

The most spectacular Chinese foreign aid project so far has been Tan-Zam, the building of the 1,100 mile railway line from Dar es Salaam, Tanzania, to Zambia. About 12,000 Chinese technicians took part in the project. Their energy became proverbial, and their modest life style won constant admiration.

By 1970 Chinese economic aid totaled about $699 million, exceeding that given by all the other Eastern countries together, including the Soviet Union. Compared to Chinese generosity, the $279.6 million given by Moscow seems rather stingy.

By 1972 twenty-six countries in Africa and Asia had received economic credits of about $1.98 billion from China. Of this amount 3 percent was loaned at 2 to 2.5 percent interest, 89 percent was interest free; and the remaining 8 percent was a gift. No other country has given help in such an extraordinary fashion.

Application to Other Developing Countries

China's policy of development aid—especially the way in which it has given credit and shared in the actual work of projects—has stirred the West to give similar help. For example, the industrialized countries revised their official credit policy in 1971 and may be on their way to doing so again.

It is particularly important for the developing countries to see how a country that is itself still developing is taking an active share in the developmental process in other countries. In the future, international solidarity in many areas may be more important than the execution of some projects that are inspired by mere nationalism.

24

CHINA AND PEACE

China's acceptance into the United Nations has changed the whole configuration of international affairs, for a bipolar world has now become tripolar. And despite the current prominence given by the press to representatives of the oil-producing countries, it is likely that it will increasingly become the spokesman for the entire Third World.

Of course, China itself is regarded by many as a threat to the rest of the world, but, as a matter of fact, China is not interested in expansion. Rather it would like to become what it once was at least in its own eyes—the "center of the world"—by influencing the minds and ideals of others. China is proud of what it has accomplished, and it is convinced that its success may be laid to new ideas and experiments, from which it hopes that others may learn. China had long been humiliated; now it has a right to regain a healthy pride in its own achievements.

Too often the Chinese way is compared to or even identified with the Russian. Yet its whole approach has been different. Even its thinking is not in the Western mould. This should put us on guard against reading our own thought patterns and our own anxieties into what it does. What we have to see when we look at China is rather the union of opposites in the totality of life and society. It is dangerous to isolate one element and stress it alone. Taken out of context it may indeed look like a threat to us, whereas when seen in tension with other elements, it manifests its creative power.

Indeed, China's greatest contribution to world peace and development may well lie in its intellectual habit of uniting opposites. As we have seen, this philosophy has grown naturally out of historical and cultural influences, for China has always had to endure tensions between uniformity and diversity within its own borders. For example, 50 to 60 percent of its land area is peopled by fifty-four national minorities, although these total only 6 percent of the whole population. Two seemingly opposed political conceptions for dealing with the variety of peoples now stand side by side: a reduction of differences and an emphasis on nationalities. Until recently, the emphasis was heaviest on eliminating differences, but at the Party Congress in late August 1973, a new, balancing emphasis was introduced: a stress on the rights of minorities.

By now one thing should have become clear to

the rest of the world: China cannot simply be equated with tyranny and the use of force. Thousands of travelers have been able to verify the fact that much of what is going on in China would long since have ended in failure without a true vision and a power flowing from within. Neville Maxwell writes: "China is driving, not driven, orchestrated, not regimented, . . . generated from within, not imparted from the top" (London *Sunday Times*, February 20, 1972).

Shortly before his death, Edgar Snow said that the Chinese experiment is very important in view of the present world situation and for any future world peace. For, if development has any connection with peace, then China has at least provided an alternative model of development. But Snow believes there is much more to be said for the Chinese model. At a time when people have begun to lose hope in the whole idea of development, China offers an example that is meaningful in itself and a source of meaning for others: a development that has profited the people, not a development that has worsened their condition.

Application to Other Developing Countries

The lesson other developing countries can learn from China is that at least there is hope for them, too.

Conclusion

CHINA AND INDIA: A CONTRAST IN DEVELOPMENT

After examining so many elements of China's model of development, in isolation and in various combinations, one can only reassemble the whole and ask, is it working? The answer, obviously, is yes, but the scope of its success can be seen only by contrasting China's development with that of another country which has chosen another model.

Of course all comparisons are dubious because each country is unique in its geography and natural resources, its past and present history, the internal and external political forces that drive it, the personalities of its leaders, and countless other factors that influence development. Nonetheless, if this *caveat* is kept in mind, comparisons can be useful tools in evaluation.

India is perhaps the best country to compare with China, because the two have chosen very different paths and because, despite vast differences, they have many characteristics in common.

Both countries are huge; indeed, each is a sub-continent. In geographic extent China is the third largest country in the world, India the seventh. And the two are the most heavily populated nations on earth. Both must cope with a population explosion and with the resultant need to stimulate the economy and the social structures that support the economy. Both are agricultural countries; at the turn of the century 85 percent of the population in each lived in small villages. And both have approximately the same amount of arable land— 271,700,000 acres in China to 308,750,00 acres in India around 1960.

In addition, both countries began independent development around the same time: India in 1947, China in 1949. Conditions at the beginning of each country's development were similar: a large population and limited space, an agricultural economy marked by a feudal proprietary system and continuous subdivision of holdings, extensive unemployment or underemployment in the agricultural sector, widespread illiteracy, inadequate roads and transportation, and few markets.

Despite these rather dismal conditions, India was actually in a far more favorable starting position than China. It certainly began its period of independence as an underdeveloped country, but also as a well-organized country with a small but functional industrial system. Its infrastructure was intact, and it had inherited an experienced administrative organization of high quality. In China, on the contrary, the entire social and economic system had been destroyed by the Japanese invasion and the Civil War. Moreover, the soil of China is generally much poorer and the climate less favorable; additionally ecological destruction was far more advanced there. Last but most important, China's available farmland had to support almost twice as many people as did India's.

India opted for Anglo-Saxon democracy and a free enterprise economy. The traditional social order was maintained and religious values continued to be influential. In addition, India was able to count on extensive help from the whole "free world." Between 1949 and 1957 the member nations of the World Bank gave India $1.3 billion in credits and grants; private sources added $280 million more. Until 1960 India's repayments were minimal.

China chose a different path, and one that Westerners often could hardly find negative enough terms to describe: for example, "a gruesome system of naked force, absolute totalitarianism, and organized want." The only help it could count on were some minimal subsidies from the Soviet Union and its satellites. Between 1949 and 1957 it received $500 million in credits from them, but during the same period had to pay the Soviet Union $700 million for services, patents, and technical advice.

Despite these drawbacks, a comparison of key figures shows that between 1950 and 1960 China's economy grew in all areas with significantly greater speed than did India's—in both absolute and per capita terms. Despite the economic devastation left by World War II and the Civil War, and despite the disturbance of the Korean War so soon after, China was back on its feet within three years after the revolution. It quickly surpassed India in all three sectors which are regarded as especially important indicators of progress in a national economy—grain production, heavy industry, and sources of energy.

Soon after 1960 it became evident that the Chinese peasants, despite that "inflexible regimentation and collectivization" so despised in the West, had not only increased the overall production of rice and wheat more quickly than their counterparts in India; they had also been quicker in learning how to protect the productivity of the soil. From the summer of 1959 to the end of 1961 one natural catastrophe followed another in China. Only in 1962 did conditions improve, but just at that moment the Soviet Union suddenly stopped supplying any kind of help. Then, in 1971 and 1972, drought struck again. Yet during these upheavals China did not suffer any famine—an extraordinary achievement for a country in which about twenty million people had starved to death as late as the 1928/29 season. Nor did the country see any phenomenon resembling India's much-feared "hunger marches" of millions of starving peasants descending upon the cities. On the contrary, during this period ten million Chinese were resettled from the cities to the rural communes.

In India, on the other hand, every year since 1965 has seen famine somewhere in the country. For example, it is estimated that during autumn 1967 in the Patna area of the Ganges Valley millions of people died of starvation.

When India became independent it was in an especially favorable situation as regards heavy industry. Steel production had been established as early as 1910, and by 1952 had grown significantly. China's heavy industry, on the other hand, was in an embryonic stage after the Civil War. The same relative situation also applied to iron ore and cement production.

The following table shows the comparative speed with which China and India were able to increase

PRODUCTION OF HEAVY INDUSTRY
(IN MILLIONS OF TONS)

| | 1952 | | 1959 | |
	India	China	India	China
iron ore	9	19	16	26
steel	1.5	1.7	2.5	13.4
cement	3.8	3.8	6.9	12.3

heavy-industry production during even the earliest years of development.

When it comes to energy sources, India has an enormous problem. For lack of other kinds of energy, the country is forced each year to burn about 3.9 billion cubic feet of firewood and about 80 million tons of cow dung (in the form of briquets). But the extensive use of wood for fires is inflicting an ever-increasing deadly blow on the forests that are ecologically so important. The use of dung for fuel rather than for fertilizer is partially responsible for India's failure to produce the 15 to 20 million tons of grain it needs to provide its people with adequate food. Yet India has done little on a large scale either to discover alternate sources of energy or to protect its ecology for the future.

China, on the other hand, has thrown itself into the work of building up the ecological infrastructure, so as gradually to gain control of nature.

An examination of most other generally accepted indicators of development shows China far ahead of India, although it started from the same point or lower. For example, all available human resources have been mobilized in China, by means of the communes. In India, unemployment in the cities and underemployment in the rural areas remains a major problem.

China has relied on human effort as an essential form of capital. India has depended on its search for credits and monetary aid for development.

China has mobilized the masses, dividing its

wealth and power ever more equally. India's social structure is manipulated by a thin upper stratum, most of whom are primarily interested in defending and advancing their own interests.

China has made agriculture the basis of its economy, while India has relied on a radical industrialization. India, therefore, provided for the training of technicians and engineers; but today it has between 50 and 70 thousand unemployed engineers and an even greater number of unemployed technicians, all of whom are unwilling to return to the villages.

The list could go on and on, but many chapters of this book have made clear China's achievements. It is sufficient to say that India can match them on very few points, especially if one looks at the situation of its entire population—not merely the privileged classes.

The best conclusion—to this comparison and to this book—is, perhaps to contrast the three main differences between present-day India and China: worldview, agricultural economy, and industry.

Today, the Chinese are inspired by a new faith and a new self-understanding. They have a vision and "a faith that moves mountains." India, on the contrary, has not been able to mobilize its masses to action; as both cause and effect, many barriers between theory and practice still exist. For example, in theory the caste system has been eliminated. But research shows that in Bombay only 3 percent, in Calcutta 6 percent, of the workers are not exposed to caste influence. Again, the traditional fatalistic philosophy of the Hindu priests and the astrologers is still prevalent among their families, avoiding any real change. In some cases land was expropriated, but the new peasant-owners had to pay compensation. Since very few peasants could do this, usually the landowners simply became money lenders. There were rural credit unions set up to help the peasants acquire expropriated land, but they failed in their purpose since, lacking political control, they fell into the hands of the traditional village dignitaries. Most often the latter collaborated with the money lenders, who required up to 72 percent interest on loans. The soil of India is gradually turning into desert. Interest in agriculture is small, and the mass exodus from the land continues. Certainly anyone who manages to acquire an education or technical skills deserts the villages and seeks a more comfortable life in the cities, despite widespread unemployment and underemployment there, even among university graduates.

Thus, at the same time as China was courageously effecting a truly radical land reform, India put off, circumvented, or even sabotaged almost all improvements. And precisely because of India's experience, the Swedish economist Gunnar Myrdal has called an effective land reform an indispensable step toward a genuine development.

In the industrial sector India is scarcely any better off. The Nagpur Resolutions concerning industry promised that the private sector would be controlled more strictly, and that care would be taken to invest capital not only in ventures that promised especially large immediate profit but also in projects needed to develop the national economy as a whole. Unfortunately, all these promises remained dead letters through the influence of bureaucratic capitalists.

From the beginning India has tried to base its development on industrialization. Yet the immense efforts India has made to industrialize have not succeeded in creating employment for the millions of job seekers. In 1966, at the end of the Third Five-Year Plan, there were officially ten million unemployed and sixteen million underemployed. (Actual figures were probably much higher.) The quality of the unemployed is fairly low: these people are illiterate, undernourished, and in poor health. Even many of the employed earn far too little to provide them with a livelihood, and undernourishment is known to be widespread among workers.

The Indian worker remains, at heart, rural, with ties still back in the village; this leads to a good deal of absenteeism. To finance trips back to the countryside for religious and family festivals, the worker must continually incur debts. One research project showed 76 percent of the industrial workers surveyed were in debt.

While industry limps along, India has seen the growth of a disproportionately large tertiary sector in its economy. Bureaucracy has taken alarming forms, and the tragic result has been conservatism. Civil servants and other functionaries are more and more opposed to any further development.

In short, all India's development planning and the $14 billion in developmental aid that poured in between its liberation and 1970 may have helped it at specific points, but the basic problems of development have hardly been touched. The poor have only become poorer and the few rich people richer.

In contrast to India, China today has eliminated hunger and unemployment. The health care given the people is modest but it is guaranteed, as are living quarters, clothing, and old-age care. Every Chinese child can learn to read and write; every Chinese child has a future and a hope. Chinese self-reliance works. Although China itself has warned others against copying it, one thing is sure: Its model of development has something to say to almost all countries.

BIBLIOGRAPHY

Mao Tse-tung. *Quotations from Chairman Mao Tse-tung*. Peking: Foreign Language Press, 1966.

———. *Selected Works*. 5 vols. New York: International Publishers, 1954–.

Moravia, Alberto. *The Red Book and the Great Wall: An Impression of Mao's China*. Translated by Ronald Strom. New York: Farrar, Straus & Giroux, 1968.

Myrdal, Jan. *Report from a Chinese Village*. Translated by Maurice Michael. New York: Pantheon, 1965.

Schram, Stuart R. *Mao Tse-tung*. Baltimore: Penguin, 1968.

———. *The Political Thought of Mao Tse-tung*. Rev. ed. New York: Praeger, 1969.

Snow, Edgar. *The Long Revolution*. New York: Random House, 1972.

———. *Red Star Over China*. Rev. ed. New York: Grove Press, 1968.

Suyin, Han. *The Morning Deluge: Mao Tsetung and the Chinese Revolution, 1893–1954*. Boston: Little, Brown, 1972.

———. *China in the Year 2001*. Harmondsworth, England: Penguin Books, 1967.